Unspun

Unspun

*Key Concepts for Understanding
the World Wide Web*

EDITED BY

Thomas Swiss

New York University Press
NEW YORK AND LONDON

NEW YORK UNIVERSITY PRESS
New York and London

Library of Congress Cataloging-in-Publication Data
Unspun : key concepts for understanding the World Wide Web /
edited by Thomas Swiss.
p. cm.
Includes bibliographical references and index.
Contents: The Web, language, and society / Thomas Swiss and
Bruce Horner — Community / Jodi Dean — Identity / Jay David
Bolter — Gender / Cynthia Fuchs — Race / Lisa Nakamura —
Political economy / Vincent Mosco — Cyberspace / Rob Shields —
Governance / Timothy S. Luke — Ideology / John M. Sloop —
Performance / Dawn Dietrich — Hypertext / Matthew G.
Kirschenbaum — Narrative / Joseph Tabbi — Authorship /
Russell A. Potter — Multimedia / Sean Cubitt.
ISBN 0-8147-9758-X (cloth : alk. paper) —
ISBN 0-8147-9759-8 (pbk. : alk. paper)
1. World Wide Web. I. Swiss, Thomas, 1952–
TK105.888 .U57 2000
004.67'8—dc21   00-010416

New York University Press books are printed on acid-free paper,
and their binding materials are chosen for strength and durability.

Manufactured in the United States of America
10 9 8 7 6 5 4 3 2 1

Contents

         Joseph Tabbi

12   Authorship   148
         Russell A. Potter

13   Multimedia   162
         Sean Cubitt

         Bibliography   187
         Contributors   199
         Index   203

Acknowledgments

Special gratitude, as always, to Cynthia, Alley, and Jacob. Thanks to Heather Bays for her help in editing this volume. To Andrew Herman; Sofia Turnbull and Nancy Smith; Joe Lenz; Dan Alexander; Ann Borel, and, especially, to all the contributors to this book: many thanks. I also wish to acknowledge the contributions of Eric Zinner, Nancy Lin, the initial reviewers of this book, my friends at New York University Press, and the Drake University Center for the Humanities.

Unspun: The Web, Language, and Society

Thomas Swiss and Bruce Horner

The World Wide Web has cut a wide path through many of our daily lives. And it is always being talked about, too—in print and on television, in movies and presidential speeches. Of course, what's being said is often simply a variation on a message that doubles as a sales pitch: "the Web changes everything." But what, exactly, is the Web changing? And how might we participate in or even direct Web-related change? These are some of the questions this collection takes up by looking at the Web as it shapes and is shaped by economic, political, social, and aesthetic forces. But there is another, somewhat different question that is at the heart of the chapters in this book. Although it does not get asked much, it's a question that is central to the study of contemporary media and culture. What are we talking about when we talk about the Web?

There are many ways to answer that question, of course, but any answer—indeed anything we can say about the Web and our experiences with it—will carry unspoken assumptions and values. It is also likely that these assumptions and values will be communicated not in technical or professional language, but in common terms like those featured in *Unspun*: community, identity, multimedia, and so on. These terms and others work so easily and well for us in our everyday lives that the ideological and historical baggage they carry is scarcely visible.

To choose an obvious example, how many times have we read or heard that the World Wide Web has sparked a "revolution"? A Web browser creates "a pathway for a global information revolution"; a university's on-line courses are part of a "revolutionary educational model." It is easy to multiply examples of this kind of talk, even though it is not at all self-evident what "revolution" involves, much less who will have benefited and what will have been changed when the "revolution" is over. Said another way, "revolution" and many other terms we use to define the substance and power of the Web embody particular cultural values and agendas that often go unconsidered. This book proposes that the "silent" assumptions behind this language be examined if we really want to know what we are talking about when we talk about the Web.

One of the aims of *Unspun*, then, is to encourage readers, especially those new to the cultural study of the Web, to ask questions about how language shapes not only our opinions of the Web but also its relationship to culture. For instance, although the popular press has always included a mix of utopian and dystopian rhetorics when reporting on the Web, in 1997—with the news full of pedophiles, pornographers, and teenage bomb-makers all using the Web—many people began to think of the Web less as an entertainment or educational site than as a sinkhole of weirdness, danger, or perversion. By 2000, however, with nearly every American business (and individuals with their home pages) having an on-line presence, and with e-commerce booming, the Web, no longer on the margins, no longer "cutting edge," was now simply another vehicle for trying to make money. As the *New York Times* recently headlined a story about "online pioneers": "The Buzz Never Stops." What are we talking about when we talk about the Web?

Of course, one of the reasons the Web is so fascinating to study right now is that the specific technology is so new that the rhetoric of and about the Web is still emerging and therefore particularly unstable, contested, in flux. Consider, for example, the automobile-age language of the Internet "information superhighway," which functioned as the dominant metaphor in the early years (1994–97) of the Web. While it enabled, shaped, and governed the widespread development and use of the Web, it has now largely faded from public view. Do our understandings and experiences of the Web, and the material construction of the Web itself, change—if only in subtle ways—as this key phrase becomes less productive in the social imagination and finally runs out of gas? And what metaphors, what kinds of hyperbole, what shifts in terms replace the exhausted rhetoric of "the highway"?

Consult the Web and you'll find new language and new spins on that language vying for attention, legitimization, and power every day.

The aim of this book is to invite readers into the range of possible ways of thinking, talking, and writing about the Web and to participate in constructing its meanings. The contributors to *Unspun* include leading scholars who have previously provided founding texts in technology-related disciplinary areas, exemplary studies of specific cases, and important essays and books linking technology, the Internet, and the Web to culture generally.

There is a companion site for this volume, located at www.nyupress .nyu.edu/unspun. The *Unspun* site contains information and links especially designed to support the themes of this book.

Chapter 1

Community

Jodi Dean

Although mediated by computers, Web-based community is infused with feeling, emotion, and affect.

Do You Want a Cookie?

Community may well be the most powerful of the aspirations linked to the World Wide Web. At a time of corporatized dislocation, rampant consumerism, inescapable spin, and a perpetually fast-forwarded pace of life, community seems to promise something simpler, richer, and more fulfilling. It evokes the friendliness of neighbors stopping by for advice or a cup of sugar, the warmth of freshly baked cookies. In a community, everybody knows your name.[1]

It's rather odd that the warm and fuzzy face-to-faceness of community would come to be associated with computer-mediated interaction—especially when we realize that a "cookie" in the Information Age is a code deposited onto our computers when we visit certain Websites, and used to facilitate e-commerce and track our Web activities. These days, the idea that everybody might know your name can be more frightening than reassuring for it suggests the increased surveillance power that the Web provides, enabling someone to find you and uncover your secrets. We tend to get our cookies unaware, uncertain of their origins, unclear about their use. On the Web, cookies come from corporations and strangers, not girl scouts and neighbors (unless they have Websites). A caring communal spirit, moreover, doesn't motivate cookie distribution. On the contrary, cookies are a fast way for companies and individuals to turn community into cash, to use our interests and fears, desires and affiliations, to sell ads, products, and data.

The double meaning of "cookies" clicks on the paradoxical link between community and computers, the ambiguity in the very meaning of community on the Web. Describing this ambiguity, the philosopher Slavoj Žižek uses the metaphor of two "dreams." The first dream is of a new populism, which "will allow individuals to band together and build a participatory grass roots political system." In the second dream, the use of computers as a tool "to rebuild community results in the building of a community *inside* the machine, reducing individuals to isolated monads, each of them alone." (1997:138–139)

Although the opposition between populism and isolation is part of the same moment, it is also usefully understood in terms of episodes or phases in the development of the World Wide Web. Community on the Web moves from a pre-Web countercultural utopia, to a more anxious and embodied notion of the community at risk in the early years of the Web, to a "killer app," or popular and profitable application, as the Web becomes commercialized in the late 1990s, to a more fleeting and contestatory ideal as the Web matures.[2]

Community, like any interesting concept, is a contested term. Indeed, the purpose of this chapter is to trace some of these contestations as they have played out on the Web. Nonetheless, it may be useful to begin with a working definition. Howard Rheingold, who has done some of the most careful thinking about computers and community, provides a helpful one: "*Virtual communities* are social aggregations that emerge from the Net when enough people carry on those public discussions long enough, with sufficient human feeling, to form webs of personal relationships in cyberspace" (1993:5). Three aspects of Rheingold's definition are worth noting. First, community is an emergent property. Community on the Web does not refer to physical communities that use computers to facilitate interaction, although physical communities often use new media, and virtual communities are often invigorated by face-to-face encounters. Rather, virtual communities involve relationships between those who are not already linked by tradition, proximity, profession, or affiliation.

Second, although mediated by computers, Web-based community is infused with feeling, emotion, and affect. Those in a virtual community understand their interactions as those of a community and hence feel a sense of obligation and responsibility to something beyond themselves. This second aspect of Rheingold's definition is important as a reminder that the coincidence of like consumption choices is not sufficient for an ascription of community. Put somewhat differently, regularly shopping at an e-commerce site or visiting the same porn site does not make consumers members of a community. Something more, something with feeling, is necessary. Finally, Rheingold suggests that a virtual community is an aggregate, a collection; it is a group compromising more than simply a few people who are already personally related to one another. Rheingold uses the term "public," implying that a virtual community has a kind of openness and accessibility that distinguishes it from more private forms of affiliation such as those in the family and workplace. Rather than emphasizing publicity, however, I find it helpful to think of this aggregate dimension of community on the Web as a reminder that "it's the group that counts." A community is more than the sum of its parts. The addition or subtraction of any single member won't make or break it (although of course an individual may have a significant impact). Thus, a Web community refers to a group integrated together by networked computers that has a sense of and a feeling toward itself as a continuing, valuable collectivity.

Counterculture, Utopia, and the Well (1971–93)

To get a sense of how radical the link between computers and community really is, recall that in the late 1960s most people thought computers were enormous, arcane, powerful, and scary machines. They associated mainframes with Big Brother and the threat of a totally controlled society. Programmers seemed like an elite priesthood capable of, if not conjuration, then at least the harnessing and manipulation of the computer's mysterious power. Students protesting the Vietnam War sometimes targeted their campus mainframes and computing departments, in part because of their perceived complicity with a war based on systems, statistics, and probability. A popular T-shirt repeated the inscription on data-entry cards and announced, "I am human being. Do not fold-spindle-mutilate."

The controlling and malevolent image of the computer started to change in the early 1970s. One site of this change was the San Francisco Bay area where antiwar activists, Berkeley dropouts, and computer buffs began experimenting with microcomputers and teaching programming to community members. In 1971, a collective of activists who wanted to use technology for social change, Resource One, secured an old XDS-940 time-share computer. They used it for mailing lists, education, and research projects (Levy 1984:164). Hoping to bring computers directly to "the people," some members of the group put together "Community Memory." With its first working terminal set up in a Berkeley record store in 1973, "Community Memory" was an electronic bulletin board that enabled users to find health clinics, exchange recipes and advice, and leave messages from make-believe and literary personas. Inspired by these possibilities of a "direct democracy of information," Stewart Brand (1974), founder and editor of the *Whole Earth Catalogue*, wrote: "Until computers come to the people we will have no real idea of their most natural functions. Up to the present their cost and size has kept them in the province of the rich and powerful institutions, who, understandably, have developed them primarily as bookkeeping, sorting and control devices. The computers have been a priceless aid in keeping the lid on top-down organization. They are splendidly impressive as oracles of (programmable) Truth, the lofty voice of unchallengeable authority" (1973:77).[3] Despite their utopian ambitions, the Community Memory group became frustrated by their unreliable equipment's frequent breakdowns and stopped the project in 1975.

Repeating the grassroots and countercultural ethos of Community Memory, BBSs (bulletin board systems) emerged in the late 1970s in Illinois and California when hobbyists connected their computers together through modems and telephone lines. The most significant virtual community to emerge with the spread and development of modem and messaging technology was The Well, Whole Earth 'Lectronic Link. The brainchild of Stewart Brand and Larry Brilliant, owner of NETI, Network Technologies International, a computer conferencing system company, The Well began in 1985 as an interactive version of Brand's magazine, the *Whole Earth Review*. Like the BBSs, The Well emphasized the autonomy of person-to-person communication, the free circulation of information, and the emancipatory potential of affiliation on the basis of common interests. Unlike the BBSs, it sought to integrate a variety of disparate concerns into one community. Whereas BBSs tended to specialize around gaming, computing,

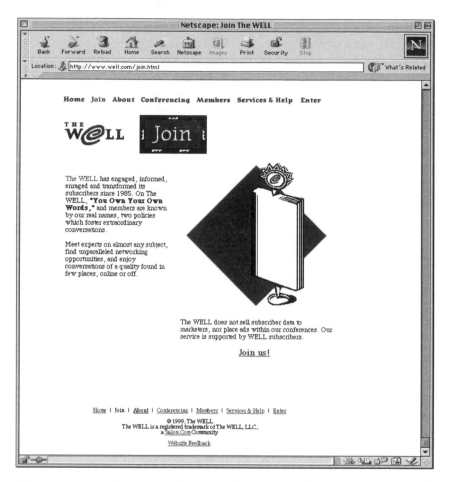

"Virtual community was considered an alternative to the impersonal, controlling forces of surveillance and economics." The Well site. http://thewell.com

and pornography, The Well brought together a broad spectrum of different people from personal computer revolutionaries to Deadheads to parents to environmentalists, giving them the opportunity to build connections beyond their particular interests. On The Well, people related on the basis of what they knew, on the information they could share, the concerns they had, and the help they could provide. Often this help was substantial, like that found among congregants in a religious community or the ideal small town: moral support for those dealing with illness and death, financial support for those lacking sufficient means.

For many, The Well, like virtual community in general, seemed to represent the dawning of a new age. It enabled connections that transcended the very limits of the body: on-line, one didn't know another's sex, race, ethnicity, or ability. One didn't respond to another on the basis of appearance, but on the basis of ideas; the virtual community was a community of mind.

Although The Well espoused a countercultural vision, staffed, in fact, by former members of a commune called the Farm and animated by the goal of providing cheap, if not free, computing and "email to the masses," it was nonetheless a business venture designed to make a profit. In order to publicize The Well, journalists were given free accounts. Heavy users and interesting participants were made "hosts" or discussion leaders, and their usage was discounted or subsidized. Matthew McClure, The Well's first director, remarked, "We needed a collection of shills who could draw the suckers into the tents" (Rheingold 1993:42). Just because The Well was countercultural, in other words, didn't mean it couldn't make a profit.

This was not the only aspect of early networked communication that pointed toward the less ideal dimensions of community.[4] Another involved surveillance and expulsion, that is, the restriction or elimination of those who disturbed community interactions. Sandy Stone describes how the ideal of unconstrained interaction destroyed another early conferencing system, CommuniTree. Striving to ensure both privacy and access in their system, the original programmers refused to change the code even after hackers repeatedly crashed the system. The system's storage disks filled up and ultimately became unreadable. The community couldn't survive. Learning from this experience, later conference software gave more power to the system operators, enabling them better to monitor, control, and, if necessary, expel uncooperative visitors. "Thus, in practice," Stone concludes, "surveillance and control proved necessary adjuncts to maintaining order in the early virtual communities" (Stone 1995:118).

Nonetheless, the ideal of community in the pre-Web period exhibited a kind of technopopulism. Virtual community was considered an alternative to the impersonal, controlling forces of surveillance and economics. Tools for the people, computers were celebrated for their ability to facilitate grassroots connection, for their capacity to revitalize connections between people and give them new opportunities to share, debate, and engage. As an alternative to the top-down control of the mainframe and the passivity-inducing effects of television, computer-mediated communication would bind people together in authentic relationships. Community was thus the promise of meaningful, personal, self-organized interconnection.

Risky Business (1985–97)

The ideals of community in the pre-Web period were powerful incentives for bringing people on-line. Yet many who ventured onto the electronic frontier discovered not the friendly and engaging free-for-all of The Well, but a whole new field of dangers and uncertainties. Instead of caring conferences of parents, they found every kind of pornography imaginable; instead of fascinating debates on politics and the economy, they found teenagers exchanging banalities and expletives; instead of information, they found drivel. Pornography and banality were already features of Usenet—an anarchic network of topic-based discussions known as newsgroups—but they were not the ideal promised by the information superhighway, much less the utopia evoked by virtual community.[5] Acknowledging that computers were enabling new forms of sociality, Clifford Stoll griped,

> But what an impoverished community! One without a church, cafe, art gallery, theater, or tavern. Plenty of human contact, but no humanity. . . what's missing from this ersatz neighborhood? A feeling of permanence and belonging, a sense of location, a warmth from local history. Gone is the very essence of a neighborhood: friendly relations and a sense of being in it together. (1995:43)

The much heralded capacity of computer-mediated communication to transcend embodied identity also came under attack as the drawbacks of malleable persona came to the fore: if we couldn't see who we were talking to, how could we trust them? How could we be sure who we were talking to? The instability of networked identities and relations was starting to look less like the fulfillment of community than its corruption.

In 1985 *Ms.* magazine published an article warning of the dangers of on-line deception. "The Strange Case of the Electronic Lover" by

Lindsy Van Gelder described the trauma experienced by subscribers to CompuServe, a commercial email and conferencing provider similar to (though less intellectual and more mainstream than) The Well, when their interactions with a caring woman, disfigured and disabled following a car crash, turned out to be exchanges with an able-bodied man, a New York psychiatrist named Alex. "Joan" had carried out long intimate conversations with many of the women she met online, occasionally encouraging her friends to have sex with her. Once "Joan" was unmasked as a construct of Alex's, many of the women who had developed close friendships with "her" felt violated. Van Gelder writes, "Even those who barely knew Joan felt implicated— and somehow betrayed—by Alex's deception. Many of us online believe that we're a utopian community of the future, and Alex's experiment proved to us all that technology is no shield against deceit" (Rheingold 1993:165).

Deception was not the only problem linked to the identity play rapidly subverting the ideal of virtual community; violence was also a threat. Liberated by the absence of the constraints of physical community, some users created extreme avatars, or net-based personalities. Extreme avatars not only shocked and disturbed those with whom they came into contact, but they also tested the limits of virtual community: was everything permitted or did community require some kind of boundary? (See "Performance," this volume.) These issues were central to the events at LambdaMOO described in an influential *Village Voice* article by Julian Dibbell. LambdaMOO was an object-oriented, multiuser database. Storing descriptions of rooms and objects, its program provided those who dialed in with the sense that they were moving through a large house. Users would present themselves as avatars who inhabited the house and interacted with other avatars. They could create and furnish their own rooms. LambdaMOO gave a virtual place to the virtual space of community.

Dibbell describes a brutal rape that took place in the living room at LambdaMOO. Mr. Bungle, "a fat, oleaginous, Bisquick-faced clown dressed in cum-stained harlequin garb" created a voodoo doll that forced legba, "a Haitian trickster spirit of indeterminate gender," to sexually service him. After Mr. Bungle was ejected from the room, the voodoo doll continued its work: legba was made to "eat his/her own pubic hair." Starsinger, a nondescript female character, was forced "to violate herself with a piece of kitchen cutlery." All the while, Mr. Bungle's laugher echoed throughout the room (Dibbell 1993:377). The problem was how to handle the situation. There were no explicit rules outlawing Mr. Bungle's behavior. The technicians and programmers overseeing the MOO, moreover, had decided not to interfere in its social life, but only to implement directives given them by the community. This meant that, in order to deal with the situation, the community would need to define itself; it would have to settle on some kind of social organization. After long debate among the victims and active participants, nothing was decided. Of his own accord, a technician intervened and "toaded," that is, killed, Mr. Bungle. When a master technician returned several days later, he intervened as well, establishing a petition system by which members could demand that recalcitrant and extreme avatars be toaded. The death penalty established the boundaries of community.

In both the "Joan/Alex" and the LambdaMOO examples, the first phase ideal of community worked as the measure against which the traumas of identity play were measured. "Joan" was a problem because she was inauthentic. Mr. Bungle's voodoo doll escapade was a crime because it challenged the meaningfulness, the real affective connection, of the LambdaMOO interactions. With the World Wide Web's initial rapid expansion in 1994, these problems of inauthenticity and meaningless became all the more striking. Where was the cyber-Eden described by WELL journalists and virtual community fans such as Brand and Rheingold? Some observers now found the very notion of virtual community implausible. Untethered by history, space, or responsibility, participants in computer-mediated communications could only simulate community. Ziauddin Sardar argued,

> A cyberspace community is self-selecting, exactly what a real community is not; it is contingent and transient, depending on a shared interest of those with the attention span of a thirty-second soundbite. The essence of real community is its presumptive perpetuity—you have to worry about other people because they will always be there. In a cyberspace community you can shut people off at the click of a mouse and go elsewhere. (1996:29)

Combined with worries about transience and disembodiment were also anxieties about embodiment. The freedoms of the Net seemed to unleash unprecedented amounts of pornography, suggesting that, far from the ideals of community, the baser dimensions of human interaction would flourish before the screens of the networked society. On July 3, 1995, *Time* magazine featured a cover article expressing these fears. Reporter Philip Elmer-Dewitt cited a controversial Carnegie-Mellon study claiming that over 80 percent of the images available on-line were pornographic. With its own shock-value graphics (one depicted a man seemingly humping a computer monitor) and hysterical tone, the article emphasized the deviance of Net-porn, the threat to children, and the movement of pornography from adult BBSs onto the Web. Moreover, it fed into congressional efforts to regulate computer networks through an extension of the Telecommunications Act of 1996 known as the Communications Decency Act.

In the second phase of Web community, the ideals that had animated the initial phase have become standards by which the ever-expanding numbers and forms of virtual interaction are judged. Computers have become tools of the people, but the people aren't using the tools to transform society in progressive directions. Rather than fulfilling community, the Web seems to threaten it as it enables people to play with identities, forfeit responsibilities, and indulge in potentially dangerous fantasies.

Making a Killing with Community

In June 1997 the U.S. Supreme Court overturned the Communications Decency Act. Two issues dominated the discussion: censorship and community standards on the one hand, and the growth of the Internet on the other. First, the Court found that the CDA was unprecedentedly broad, effectively regulating email exchanges, discussions of safe sex, and even library card catalogs. It explained that the community standards component of the test for obscenity "when applied to the Internet means that any communication available to a nationwide audience will be judged by the standards of the community most likely to be offended by the message" (Section VII). The Internet, in other words, should not be thought of as a community or judged by the standards of community. The Net was, or had the potential to be, much bigger and more inclusive than any community. The small-town ideals of face-to-faceness and civility were simply too restrictive for such a broad-based and inclusive medium. Second, in their support of regulations of obscene and indecent material on the

Internet, the government had argued that the vast amount of pornography in cyberspace was hindering the growth of the World Wide Web. The Court was not convinced and in fact took the opposite position. It emphasized that from the outset the Telecommunications Act was designed to promote the development of, and competition within, the telecommunications market by reducing regulation. The CDA, in contrast, was a regulatory effort. The Court noted further the District Court's finding that credit card verification systems could prove burdensome to Internet content providers and prohibitively expensive for commercial as well as noncommercial Websites. In short, the regulations proposed by the CDA were likely to inhibit not simply communication among adults but the economic development of the Web as well. With its decision that the CDA was too commercially restrictive for the fast lane on the information superhighway, the Court established a space for e-commerce and business use of the Web.

The Court's overturning of the CDA reset the terms of community in the Web's third phase. Rather than being held to the idealistic standards of the first phase, computer-mediated interaction appeared as a commercial venture and economic ideal. In this setting, the Net was not to be judged by the norm of community but by that of the "killer app" designed to increase the stickiness of Websites (their ability to attract users and get them to stay, click through, and return). As Katie Hafner observes in her history of The Well, the

> idea of The Well is in some ways more potent than the actuality. Most Internet entrepreneurs seeking to create a similar community (that is, create a place that will get people to keep coming back) have never actually been on The Well. The image they have of it is formed from a few fabled incidents, such as The Well's outpourings of help and concern in the face of illness. . . . These entrepreneurs brandish the term community building as if it is a simple matter of putting up a chat space on a Web site (1997:29).[6]

One of the important initial commercial framings of Web-based community was offered by two consultants from McKinsey and Company, John Hagel and Arthur Armstrong. Their book, *Net Gain*, argued that community should be part of every plan to do business on and through the Web. Community, in other words, could be converted into capital. They echoed an idea already manifest by hosting services such as America Online, CompuServe, and Prodigy. But they also extended it by associating community with site stickiness in general. Put somewhat differently, what the emphasis on community as a marketing concept meant was that any site—whether it provided extensive chat or conferencing services or not—could be the locus of community. By the late 1990s, then, Web magazines, professional resource centers, information portals, and merchants were all positioning themselves as communities. There were communities of Nerf-fans and beer drinkers, of X-Philes and auction addicts. Consumption, it seemed, provided a commonality of feeling and identification sufficient to warrant the attribution of community.

To be sure, important benefits attached themselves to the new thinking about community. First, local physical communities were more likely to use the Web to keep their constituencies up-to-date and to give them a vehicle for expressing their concerns. Second, professional organizations were able to increase communication among their members, providing them with easily accessible databases, discussion opportunities, and virtual homes. Finally, computer users as well as professionals were able to stretch and morph Web technologies so as to undertake previously inconceivable types of interaction. More fleeting, short-term discussions emerged as momentary enactments of community. Opportunities to provide product reviews and feedback—as on Amazon.com—suggested larger networks of interest and response. The very effort to provide information to anyone who might come searching for it suggested possibilities of, if not exactly care, then at least connection. They might not have been The Well— but then neither was The Well itself.

Contesting Community

The commerce-based view of community that has arisen with the phenomenal growth of the Web has been a disappointment to many who had hoped that computer-mediated interaction would eliminate political control and societal atomism. Fortunately, the story doesn't stop here; as the new millennium begins, the conversations, links, and possibilities enabled by the Web point toward some of the same contestatory potential longed for by the pre-Web counterculture. E-commerce and on-line auctions provide some consumers with opportunities to undercut market prices. New media, like MP3, subvert hierarchies such as those that have structured the recording industry; artists can go directly to the people. And activists are able to organize opposition rapidly and spread word of important issues and events.

The warmth may not be there. The continuity of attachment may be lacking. Self-interest may usually override a feeling of commonality. But the sense of being part of something larger does accompany community on the Web. You just have to be careful where you get your cookies.

NOTES

1. This is the notion of community idealized by John Perry Barlow in his influential essay, "Is There a There in Cyberspace?" available at www.eff.org/pub/Publications/John_Perry_Barlow/utne_community.article.

2. I take the expression "killer app" from Theresa Senft, "Baud Girls and Cargo Cults," in *Magic, Metaphor, and Power: The World Wide Web and Contemporary Cultural Theory*, ed. Andrew Herman and Thomas Swiss (New York: Routledge, 2000.)

3. See also Theodore Roszak, *The Cult of Information* (New York: Pantheon, 1986), 138–141; and Leslie Regan Shade, *Gender and Community in the Social Constitution of the Internet* (Ph.D. dissertation submitted in Communications at McGill University, Montreal, 1997), 104–107.

4. One of the first people kicked off The Well was a Berkeley grandmother who went by the name Mark Ethan Smith. See Hafner 1997.

5. For accounts of community in Usenet groups, see Margaret L. McLaughlin, Kerry K. Osborne, and Christine B. Smith, "Standards of Conduct on Usenet," 90–111; Richard C. MacKinnon, "Searching for the Leviathan on Usenet," 112–137; and Nancy K. Baym, "The Emergence of Community in Computer-Mediated Communication," 138–163, all in *CyberSociety: Computer-Mediated Communication and Community*, ed. Steven G. Jones (Thousand Oaks, Calif.: Sage, 1995).

6. Archive version available at www.wired.com.

Chapter 2

Identity

Jay David Bolter

The personal homepage, whose purpose is nothing other than identity construction, has already emerged as one of the most interesting Web genres.

As many media critics have recognized, we see ourselves today in and through the available media. When we look at a traditional photograph or a perspective painting, we understand ourselves as the reconstituted station point of the photographer or the artist. When we watch a film or a television broadcast, we identify with the changing point of view of the camera. When we put on a virtual-reality headset, we become the focus of an elaborate technology for real-time, three-dimensional graphics and motion tracking. The World Wide Web, too, permits us to construct our identities in and through the sites that we create as well as those that we visit.

This is not to say that our identity is fully determined by media, but rather that we employ media in defining both our personal and our cultural identities. Because media are simultaneously technical analogs and social expressions of our identity, we become simultaneously both the subject and object of our contemporary media. We are that which the film, television, or Web camera is trained on; at the same time, we become the camera itself. This is not an entirely new phenomenon. Older, verbal media continue to serve this function of identification as well. We continue to define ourselves through characterizations in popular written fiction and in news, fashion, and leisure magazines—to identify with the voices in which those written

narratives are told. New media such as the Web simply offer new opportunities for self-definition. We can now identify with the vivid
graphics and digitized videos of Web pages or computer games as
well as the swooping perspective of virtual reality systems and of
digitally generated film and television logos.

We always understand a particular medium in relation to other
past and present media forms. When we watch the filmed adaptation
of a novel, we bring to the film a notion of self appropriate to the
written prose form of the novel. When we experience a virtual reality
application, our digital point of view is understood as a refashioning
of the point of view that we have occupied for decades in film and
television and for centuries in photographs and paintings. When we
run a multimedia program on our desktop computer, each windowed
space (containing prose, static graphics, or digitized video) may offer
a different mediation of the subject. Because we understand media
through the ways in which they challenge and reform other media,
we understand our mediated selves as reformed versions of earlier
mediated selves. Whenever our identity is mediated in this way, it is
also "remediated"—reconstructed and refashioned from earlier
media forms. This process of refashioning is also at work in the identity constructions of the World Wide Web.[1]

Consuming Identities

In the second half of the 1990s, the World Wide Web became commercialized and developed rapidly as a channel for consumer culture. In
earlier media forms—particularly magazines as well as radio, television
programs, and commercials—the individual reader, listener, or viewer
is constructed as a consumer, whose wants and needs are defined in
terms that particular products can satisfy. Commercial aspects of the
World Wide Web have continued this tradition. As soon as it became
possible to insert graphics along with text on a Web page, designers of
Websites set out to fashion the Web according to the principles of
graphic design that had prevailed in print since the 1930s and the advent of the so-called International style. Especially in the United States,
this system of graphic design was inextricably associated with corporate commercial advertising. Its goals were to define a unique graphic
identity for the corporation and to position the viewer as a consumer of

the corporation's goods and services. Websites have developed their own version of the magazine ad: the so-called banner, which can be inserted into all sorts of information and entertainment pages and which encourages the visitor to "click through" to the advertiser's site. The visitor then becomes a consuming unit, whose appetites are calculated in terms of hits and click-throughs.

As streaming media become more broadly available, the Web expands its representations of the consumer. The Web can move beyond static graphic design to define the consumer through audiovisual displays of products and services. Television-like commercials can appear on the Web, defining the Web viewer, like the television viewer, as a curious and acquisitive eye. Beyond overt advertising, the Web has the capacity to refashion the entire spectrum of the entertainment industry and so to appropriate that industry's powers to influence contemporary culture. WebTV is one example of the way in which the World Wide Web may converge with conventional television. Meanwhile, traditional Websites provide fans with supplemental information about their favorite television shows, while the film industry promotes new releases through sites that offer on-line trailers, games, and contests. The Web has also converged with the music industry by permitting users to hear excerpts of popular music and then to purchase the CD or to download the digitized music directly into a player.

In all these cases, the Web is reaffirming the construction of the individual as a consumer of popular culture. The question is whether the Web's construction of the consumer differs from the construction offered through earlier media forms. Television, radio, and magazines, being mass media, must define the consumer's identity in very general terms. Even when a television program or magazine is targeted to a particular demographic group, the audience is still measured in the hundreds of thousands or millions. According to some business people and economists, the Web's great advantage is that it can gather information about the individual user and therefore tailor its commercial messages much more specifically. By tracking and recording the characteristics and preferences of the individual user, a Website can decide which banners or pages to show. A user who clicks to the sports section of a news and information site may receive banner ads for television sports broadcasts or perhaps even for beer and other products associated with sports viewing. If a user visits an on-line bookstore and makes several purchases, on subsequent visits to that site she may receive recommendations about new books of special interest to her. Although the practice is controversial, some Web companies may even sell such information to other companies, so that Web consumers begin to take on identities that follow them in their journeys through cyberspace. In these ways, the Web promises to refine the techniques of demographic targeting and therefore to complete the task of defining the individual in a mass culture through patterns of consumption.

The Homepage

If the Web offers any hope that it will go beyond the identification of the individual as consumer, that hope would seem to lie in the ways in which individual users can "talk back" on the Web. Unlike television or magazines, for example, where opportunities for broadcasting or publication are limited, the Web is a media form in which the individual can take on the role of producer as well as consumer. Admittedly, most people who browse the Web do not have the skills or inclination to create their own sites. Nevertheless, there are hundreds of thousands of personal sites on the Web, and these sites have the same status as the biggest and the most elaborately funded commercial sites: all are reachable by typing a URL (Uniform Resource Locator) or Web address into a browser. Individuals and small groups who could never afford to buy time on commercial television or to publish their own magazine, can project their identity on the Web. And the personal homepage, whose purpose is nothing other than identity construction, has already emerged as one of the most interesting Web genres.

The new genre of the homepage does have precedents in other media. The homepage is a combination of earlier verbal or visual forms, including the résumé, the portfolio, and even in some cases the autobiographical sketch. Many homepages are simply electronic versions of the business résumé. Such sites can also serve as portfolios when the individual works in new media design or in a related field, such as graphics, architecture, or industrial design. Beyond the résumé, however, the homepage offers the opportunity for seemingly unlimited self-representation—the opportunity to publish oneself to a potential audience of millions. In fact, homepages often play with or against the apparent anonymity of publication on the Web. Because publication is merely a matter of creating Web pages and loading them on to a server, many individuals seem to feel little constraint about revealing copious and intimate details of their lives. Many sites feature material that could be of interest only to the creator herself: baby pictures of the creator or pictures of her cat.

The homepage thus blurs the distinction between the public and the private, and this blurring also has antecedents in earlier media. In the medium of print, as Elizabeth Eisenstein has argued (1979:230–231), the personal essay, as pioneered by Montaigne and other Renaissance writers, and the autobiography were simultaneously public and private forms: they painted an intimate portrait of the author and yet published that portrait to thousands of anonymous readers. The Web seems to magnify the power of these earlier forms by handing it over to a larger group of authors and by making possible almost instant publication to a much larger audience. The Website Yahoo! (www.yahoo.com December 18, 1999) currently lists almost fifty thousand homepages, and this number must represent only a small fraction of such sites.

Webcams

Webcams constitute perhaps the most extreme form of self-projection available through the Web. In this genre, an image produced by a video camera is digitized and inserted into a Web page. Usually, a Webcam presents a freeze-frame from a video stream; this frame is updated at intervals ranging from a few seconds to a few hours. Some Webcams, however, now stream continuously over the Web, and may even offer audio as well. Webcams may be pointed at anything from a person's pet hamster to a busy highway, a mountaintop, or, in the case of NASA Webcams, the surface of Mars. They make some portion of the world available in cyberspace. Webcams refashion the work and cultural significance of close-circuit surveillance cameras as well as live television broadcasts, and appear to offer the viewer greater control of her view than these earlier technologies. On the Web, she can choose among thousands of such sites now available, and in a few cases she can even control the movement of the camera.

Webcams maintained by individuals or small groups are exercises in the redefinition and projection of identity. They radically extend the process that individual homepages have begun. Many young people, college students in particular, have set up Webcams in their dorm rooms or apartments. Some leave the cameras on day and night, so that all their activities are broadcast across cyberspace. Some Webcams are set up to monitor a group of young people living together, and at least one such site (www.hereandnow.net) is commercial. Such sites subvert the traditional or expected separation between the public and the private to a greater degree than ordinary homepages. They become, above all, claims to celebrity by their owners.

For decades, sociologists and cultural critics have suggested that the contemporary media, particularly television, both intensify and trivialize the notion of celebrity. The media pique our curiosity by providing more and more details about the "rich and famous," while occasionally designating "ordinary" people (especially those who have experienced some personal tragedy) for this same treatment. The new genre of Webcams allows individuals to bypass that selection process and designate themselves as celebrities. Personal Webcams refashion pseudodocumentary television programs (such as "The Real World" on MTV), in which cameras have been trained on families or groups of students over a period of days or months. Again, the Webcam "democratizes" this television genre by allowing anyone to become the subject of her own documentary.

Consciously or not, individuals who put their lives on the Web are performing rituals of narcissism that have been associated with video art (of, for example, Nam June Paik and Vito Acconci) by critics such as Rosalind Krauss. They are suggesting that their identity can be captured in digitized video streams and projected through this new media form. Like performance artists, they are willing to turn their own lived environment into a media form. Webcam identity is realized through total media saturation, a stream of unedited and potentially endless images or video clips. It is a series of poses or character positions that the subject may assume consciously, or only semiconsciously, as the fact of being continuously on camera becomes second nature to her. Although they make up only a small fraction of the hundreds of thousands or millions of sites, Webcams nevertheless constitute a paradigm for the construction of (postmodern) identity on the Web.

Digital Media and Postmodern Identity

In 1991 Kenneth Gergen noted in the *Saturated Self* that television and radio

> saturate us with the voices of humankind—both harmonious and alien.
> . . . Social saturation furnishes us with a multiplicity of incoherent and
> unrelated languages of the self. For everything we "know to be true"
> about ourselves, other voices within respond with doubt and even deri-
> sion. This fragmentation of self-conceptions corresponds to a multiplic-
> ity of incoherent and disconnected relationships. These relationships
> pull us in a myriad of directions, inviting us to play such a variety of
> roles that the very concept of an "authentic self" with knowable charac-
> teristics recedes from view. (1991:6–7)

If television and radio lead to saturations (and remediations) of the
self, electronic forms such as homepages and Webcams as well as
email, newsgroups, chatrooms (often now accessed through the
Web), and textual virtual environments (MUDs and MOOs usually
accessed separately from the Web) carry the process further. Unlike
television and radio, these digital media allow the reader to write or
talk back and so to establish a reflexive relationship that characterized some earlier writing technologies. Teachers of writing have discovered that these synchronous and asynchronous applications are
ideal for the ongoing redefinition of the self. Almost the sole purpose
of chatrooms and MUDs is the construction of and experimentation
with the user's identity. Those who participate in these electronic environments are suggesting a new set of cultural uses for the computer
and a new metaphor by which to understand this machine. (See
"Multimedia," this volume.)

For decades after the computer's invention in the 1940s, American
culture drew comparisons between the computer and the reasoning
human mind. The computer science discipline of artificial intelligence, which flourished from the 1950s through the 1980s, proceeded
from the conviction that the human mind was in essence a program
running on the "wetware" of the brain and could therefore be imi-
tated and ultimately surpassed by software running on digital machines. Computer scientists and psychologists who worked in artificial intelligence emphasized the analytical, the rational, and the
transparent aspects of the human mind. However, MUDs, MOOs,

and chatrooms change the terms of the metaphor. At least with their current interfaces, these electronic environments do not seem well suited to complex or abstract discussion. Spontaneous, playful, and personal, these technologies seem to lend themselves more readily to the construction of the self as a social agent than as a reasoning machine. In writing about the cultural significance of these communications technologies, educators talk about the self rather than the mind.

In *Life on the Screen* (1995), Sherry Turkle examined how the regular participants in MUDs created and elaborated their identities. A MUD (or MOO) is a collaborative, networked environment in which each participant assumes a name and provides a prose description of herself. The MUD itself consists of a number of connected rooms or other spaces, each of which may have its own associated description. Each participant can communicate with others in the same room by typing messages at her keyboard. The messages normally appear on the screens for all the participants to read. All the participants' characters contribute to a collective play script or novel. In fact, a MUD is an electronic remediation of the printed novel, with its mixture of narrative and descriptive passages, while a chatroom remediates a play script, in which dialogue between the characters constitutes almost the entire text. The claim that these remediations make to heightened authenticity of experience is that they are collaborative and spontaneous. Each participant contributes the dialogue and third-person narrative for her character, as this extract from an on-line "wedding" indicates:

> Tarniwoof says, "At the engagement ceremony you gave one another an item which represents your love, respect and friendship for each other."
>
> Tarniwoof turns to you.
> Tarniwoof says, "Achilles, do you have any reason to give your item back to Winterlight?"
> Winterlight attends your answer nervously.
> You would not give up her gift for anything.
> Tarniwoof smiles happily at you.
> Winterlight smiles at you. (Turkle 1995:195)

Like the traditional nineteenth- or twentieth-century novel, the MUD is about the definition and maturation of character. However, the MUD greatly magnifies the polyvocality of the printed novel. For in reading a traditional novel by a single author, we know that all the characters really speak with one authorial voice, no matter how much that voice may be modulated and disguised. When we join a MUD, however, we know that the polyvocality, and sometimes the cacophony, is real, because the authorship is shared by many participants. Moreover, each participant in a MUD may choose to change her identity by assuming a different name and providing a different description. Each networked user may also belong to several MUDs and chatrooms and have different identities in each one. In the age of print, we have regarded writing as a process of assuming multiple, differently modulated voices—one for personal letters, one for business communications, one for scholarly publications, and so on. The networked environments of MUDs and chatrooms multiply the opportunities for identity assumption while also greatly diminishing the obstacles and the potential dangers of assuming false and conflicting identities. In a textual environment such as a MUD or chatroom, no one can verify a participant's age or gender. In particular, women often assume male identities and the reverse (Bruckman 1999). The combination of network connections, which allow participants to communicate in "real time," and the textual mode of communication has given American culture a perfect artifact with which to ring changes on the construction of postmodern identity. As Sherry Turkle puts it: "Internet experiences help us to develop models of psychological well-being that are in a meaningful sense postmodern: They admit multiplicity and flexibility. They acknowledge the constructed nature of reality, self, and other" (1995:263).

In one sense a MUD is structured like a traditional hypertext with its predetermined nodes and links: the rooms of the MUD constitute the nodes that participants visit, and the doors or passageways between rooms constitute the links. Within each room, however, the dialogue is neither predetermined nor under the control of a single author, so that the MUD remediates the printed novel in a way different from the classic hypertexts of Michael Joyce and others. (See "Hypertext," this volume.) Nevertheless, the MUD remains hypertextual in its claims of flexibility and indeterminacy. Like the global hypertext of the World Wide Web, a MUD generally operates over the Internet, and communications links between the participants are like the links between the pages of the Web. A MUD seeks to fulfill the promise of what Michael Joyce (1995:39–59) has called "constructive hypertext," offering its participants a site for defining a networked self or indeed a whole series of networked selves.

Our contemporary electronic culture is exploiting MUDs and chatrooms, together with various genres of Websites, in order to promote a postmodern sense of identity—different from the stable, single, and unitary identity that has constituted a Western ideal in the past. That ideal was appropriate to an age of print, in which the autobiography and the Bildungsroman recorded the achievement of a unified identity and character. Again, this is not to say that the technology of print determined this cultural ideal. A variety of intersecting philosophical, social, economic, and technical forces converged around that ideal. The concept of the autonomous ego, capable of establishing its rational view of an objective world, is often associated with the triumph of Cartesian philosophy in the seventeenth century. Descartes wanted to secure an epistemological and psychological foundation for his observations of the world. In a sense Cartesian philosophy found in the printing press a technology of representation that could record and reflect the stability that Descartes sought in human nature.

Today, the Cartesian demand for psychological unity and autonomy has largely been rejected in favor of a fluid cognitive psychology that is often characterized as postmodern. The Web and associated Internet technologies, together with television and radio, provide us with genres and forms that suit our preference for multiple, shifting, and highly mediated representations of identity. A networked self is displacing the Cartesian and printed self as a cultural paradigm. This networked self is organized like the Web itself, as a constantly changing set of affiliations or links. At any given moment, an individual is defined by the connections that she chooses to establish with other individuals, activity groups, and religious and secular organizations. She is, in principle, always free to break these connections and establish new ones, just as in a MUD she is always free to change her description and become a different character. The fluidity of electronic identity has implications for electronic community. (See "Community," this volume.) The networked self of the World Wide Web, MUDs, and chatrooms seems to correspond to a fluctuating and relatively weak notion of community, because in cyberspace identity and community are defined reciprocally. If electronic identity is now constituted as the set of links radiating out from an individual user, then a community is simply the sum of all the users joined by a particular set of links at a particular moment. Each Internet user belongs to many such communities, and she joins new communities and leaves old ones easily. Her identity is a series of snapshots or "screen dumps," each of which represents a particular constellation of affiliations that make sense for her at the moment.

Embodied Identity

What contemporary cultural theorists disliked most about the Cartesian philosophy of the self was its rigid distinction between mind and body. By insisting that the essence of the self was the reasoning mind, Cartesians were denying the importance of the body in constructing our identities. Descartes sought the human essence and identity in his famous withdrawal from the embodied world. In this withdrawal, he had to discount any markers of identity that are now central to cultural theory, such as race, gender, and economic class. The question now is whether electronic technologies like the World Wide Web continue in the Cartesian tradition: do they disembody the user and therefore cut her off from the racial, gendered, and other social roots of her identity? Some cyberenthusiasts, among them John Perry Barlow, have made precisely this claim as an advantage of the networked self. They have argued that in these new communications technologies race, gender, and even many physical disabilities do not matter: in cyberspace women and minorities can communicate without experiencing the prejudices that they confront in the physical world. (See "Gender," this volume.)

Contemporary cultural theorists argue that this claim is utterly wrongheaded—above all, because the cultural markers of the body are not erased in cyberspace. As Allucquere Roseanne Stone put it, "Cyberspace developers foresee a time when they will be able to forget about the body. But it is important to remember that virtual community originates in, and must return to, the physical. . . . Forgetting about the body is an old Cartesian trick" (1991:113). Our embodied identities intrude subtly or blatantly in the Web pages that we construct and in the conversations we have in MUDs and chatroom. We import the cultural markers of the body into cyberspace, even when we cannot see our fellow MUD and chatroom participants. Although we cannot be sure of the gender of various MUD characters, we still behave differently toward female characters than we do toward male ones. Cyberspace simply becomes another arena for the complex social negotiations of our culture. Cultural theorists argue that we can never truly erase markers such as race and gender because they constitute our identity. An attempt to erase them ends up making norms out of the dominant race, gender, or social groups in our society. If cyberspace could become the home of pure Mind, as some cyberenthusiasts suggest, it would simply be the home of a parochially Cartesian (that is, white, male, Eurocentric) version of the self. (See "Race," this volume.)

In any case, electronic technologies of communication cannot ultimately deny our embodied identities. Instead, our culture is using these technologies to examine the meaning of embodiment—to explore how we choose to represent our embodied identities to others and ourselves. Many contemporary cultural practices (including medical prosthetics, diet regimes, plastic surgery, cosmetics, and body art) treat the body as a field for creative manipulation. No longer satisfied with the bodies with which they were born, many individuals now choose to express themselves through such manipulations. The electronic networked self is another of these cultural practices, for it too supports a fluid and manipulable definition of embodied identity. In a MUD or chatroom, we do not forget our bodies; rather, we represent our bodies to other participants either through textual descriptions or in some cases through digitized images. These represented bodies are entirely under their users' control. Other participants in the MUD or chatroom can only operate with the textual or visual evidence that a user chooses to give them. Thus, in electronic environments, embodiment in all its aspects (physical appearance, race, gender, economic class, and often even physical location) is more malleable than it ever is in the physical world. The malleability of the body contributes significantly to the fluid sense of identity in electronic environments.

NOTES

1. The idea that new digital media work by refashioning or "remediating" older media was developed by me in collaboration with Richard Grusin in our coauthored book: *Remediation: Understanding New Media*, published by

MIT Press. Portions of this article were based on chapters 15, 16, and 17 of that book, passages of which are reprinted with the kind permission of MIT Press. Other passages in this article have been taken from the second edition of my book, *Writing Space*, to be published by Lawrence Erlbaum, and are reprinted with the kind permission of Lawrence Erlbaum Associates.

Chapter 3

Gender

Cynthia Fuchs

Even as gender on the Web may be mobile, excessive, or rebellious, it also—like gender in "real life"—sets limits, encodes behaviors and signs, and defines desires.

Gender is always a relationship, not a preformed category of beings or a possession that one can have. Gender does not pertain more to women than to men. Gender is the relation between variously constituted categories of women and men (and variously arrayed tropes), differentiated by nation, generation, class, lineage, color, and much else.
—Donna Haraway, *Modest_Witness@Second_ Millenium.FemaleMan_Meets_OncoMouse: Feminism and Technoscience,* p. 28

If we think of the body not as a product but as a process—and embodiment as an effect—we can begin to ask questions about how the body is staged differently in different realities. Virtual environments offer a new arena for the staging of the body—what dramas will be played out in virtual worlds?
—Anne Balsamo, *Technologies of the Gendered Body: Reading Cyborg Women,* p.131

Gender is just a doorway, and so is sexuality, race and age. What "it" boils down to is the nature of identity and relationships. How can we connect in a world that wants to keep us apart?
—Kate Bornstein, http://www.ctheory.com/ a-kate_bornstein.html

Gender is notoriously hard to define. It is produced by cultures, shaped by historical conditions, and altered by power dynamics. It is, as Donna Haraway observes, a relationship. In most cases, this is a relationship between bodies: your own and someone else's. But it is also a relationship between yourself and your body, or your idea of yourself and your idea of someone else. It is a relationship that is never quite stable, that changes over time and under shifting circumstances.

This relationship—or more accurately, this set of relationships—has everything to do with your sense of identity: the identity you are assigned at birth (indicated, for instance, by pink or blue baby blankets), the identity marked by your genitals, the identity determined by other people's perceptions of you, the identity you assume or imagine for yourself, the identity you perform daily or intermittently, the identity that depends on your sexual behaviors, desires, and inclinations. Gender is simultaneously performance and desire, conformity and resistance, pathology and power; it is a series of moments, a precarious and mutating aspect of who you think you might be. Gender is discontinuous and uncertain, and as technologies expand our abilities to shapeshift and imagine our "selves," gender is increasingly difficult to perceive and easy to put on.

Gender on the Web and the Internet is both more of the same and something else again. Given the enormous possibilities for performance and projection in electronic and digital venues, for dislocations from visible and material bodies, gender is cast as new, ever more evanescent relationships. According to many accounts—by MOO and MUD participants, by email subscribers, and by game players—the Web allows and even encourages sundry acts of passing and drag, seduction and persuasion. Such acts can be innovative and transgressive, elusive and illusive, or conformist and predictable; they raise questions concerning identity, community, faith, trust, and intimacy. Because gender on the Web is precisely not physical, it demands self-identification and presentation, versatility and stylization. Above all, it privileges imagination. Furthermore, because it is acted and discerned deliberately, gender on the Web is both collapsed onto and distinct from sexuality and sexual interests.

For these reasons, gender on the Web is often volatile and disturbing. This chapter examines such volatility and disturbance, while also looking at the ways in which gender on the Web develops its own conventions, rituals, and expectations rendered through patterns of behavior, appearance, and language. But even as gender on the Web may be

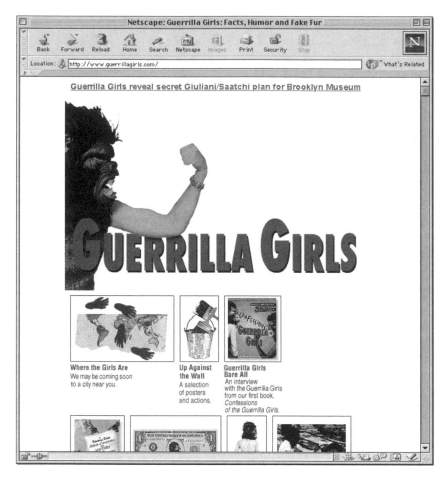

"Because gender on the Web is precisely not physical, it demands self-identification and presentation, versatility and stylization." The cybergrrl.com site. http://www.guerillagirls.com

mobile, excessive, or rebellious, it also—not unlike gender in "real life"—sets limits, encodes behaviors and signs, and defines desires.

Gender on the Web is represented and refracted in multiple ways, having to do with academic culture (as in "women's studies"), sexuality (as in debates over pornography and censorship), and community (as in the "gender community"), which early put the Web and Internet to use for organizing, discussing, and raising awareness of transgender and transsexual experiences. (See "Community," this volume.) The sheer number and diversity of sites and discussions afforded to any of these broad categories attest to the significance of gender—as concept and predicament—on the Web.

Transcending Gender

Transcending gender—indeed, transcending any identity determined by physical attributes, including race, age, and disability—is the great unfulfilled and unfulfillable promise of the Web. When William Gibson envisioned the character Case's extrabody cyber experiences in his novel *Neuromancer* (1984), he articulated the desires of many prospective Web surfers and inhabitants. (See "Cyberspace," this volume.) Gibson imagined a world where any bodies that could be conceived could also be lived in, at least for a short while. Authentic selves, housed in born-with bodies, became nostalgic notions, prepostmodern illusions. Now, with Case jacked in and riding along "inside" Molly's mobile and technologically enhanced body, the question of who is feeling what and how such feelings determined or are determined by gender become exponentially more complicated.

Donna Haraway (1991) theorized gender in a vitally new way in her groundbreaking and much anthologized essay, "A Cyborg Manifesto." In Haraway's heady mix of organism and machine, fiction and lived experience, she clarifies the ways in which communication and information technologies might affect a redistribution of knowledge, energy, and power. In Haraway's analysis, "Gender, race, or class consciousness is an achievement forced on us by the terrible historical experience of the contradictory social realities of patriarchy, colonialism, and capitalism" (1991:155). The cyborg, she writes, is a "creature in a post-gender world; it has no truck with bisexuality, pre-oedipal symbiosis, unalienated labor, or other seductions to organic wholeness through a final appropriation of all the powers of the parts into a higher unity" (1991:150).

Such a "postgender" world seems almost possible on the Web, where disembodied experience is the rule rather than the exception. And this was and remains the crux of the Web's early commercial and cultural appeals; if you can imagine it, you can be it on the Web, however hybrid, unruly, or confusing. Haraway's dream quickly became a rallying point for Web makers and consumers, demonstrated in part by the many Web pages that pay tribute to her work. Many of these pages entail discussions and essays about Haraway's cyborg theories, in the explicate-and-celebrate mode. The cyborg's allure is easy to understand: it represents a third term in an otherwise binary system of comprehension and meanings, the not-male and not-female, the not-human and not-machine. The cyborg embodies irony and integration, a kind of writing and self-imagining, a tool to "reverse and displace the hierarchical dualisms of naturalized identities," a means to a "powerful infidel heteroglossia" (1991:175, 181). Haraway complicates the dichotomy of male and female by adding the third, unfixed and unfixable term, the cyborg, into the continuum of definitions from human to machine: if one is not quite human, how can one be assigned a single gender? And if one is not quite machine, how can one avoid being gendered? "The cyborg," she writes, "is a condensed image of both imagination and material reality, the two joined centres of any possibility of historical transformation" (1991:150).

Taking Haraway's assertion that the "cyborg is a creature in a post-gender world," as her point of departure for her essay, "Computers and the Communication of Gender," Elizabeth Lane Lawley writes, "This vision encourages us to take advantage of the instabilities in boundaries that new technologies expose, and provides us with a conceptual framework for shedding the essentialist linking of biological body and gendered expectations. What remains is a movement from Haraway's physical cyborg body to the virtual self created through communication technology" (http://www.itcs.com/elawley/gender.html).

These visions—of a postgender world and virtual selves—have led Haraway's followers and other optimists to imagine a sort of utopian moment when virtual selves may exist beyond the present limitations of embodied differences, mutations, and oppressions. The cyborg has certainly inspired repeated (and alternately imaginative and tiresome) riffs: these include familiar stories about valiant warriors and enigmatic tricksters, as well as drag personas and interactive appearances. But in any of these instances, gender is not so much transcended as it is reconfirmed as a set of behaviors and expectations, recognizable and readable by audiences. (See "Ideology," this volume.) As Haraway reminds us, "a cyborg's body is not innocent" (1991:180). It is, instead, a deliberate and well-staged metaphor that enables both performers and audiences to destroy previous myths and build new ones.

Performing Gender

As theorists from Judith Butler to Sherry Turkle to Allucquere Roseanne Stone have argued, we perform gender daily, and while its performance in virtual environments might be exacerbated or altered, it is not necessarily radically different. Moreover, gender is a relationship. Any radical change might leave the audience—the other part of the relationship—out of the construction. You know you are male or female, you assume masculine or feminine characteristics, you follow the codes to make sense of yourself for your audience. For the twelve-year-old tomboy or Zack Hanson look-alike, for the Spice Girl wannabe or next Mia Hamm, the codes are generally loose: today, girls and boys can easily wear similar hair, costumes, and other gender cues. On-line, where children are learning early to perform identity—as it is gendered, aged, raced, sexed, and classed—there is even more room for play and transformation. And such activities need not be deceptive or mean-spirited, any more than performing gender via (stereo)typically femme mall-bought clothing and accessories.

As Turkle (1995, 1997) notes, "virtual gender-swapping" can be a game or a way to try out a new identity without the risks that accompany such experimental self-displays in real life. It is also, as has been noted in the many stories about deception, abuse, or harassment on-line, commonly a means for prosaic power tripping without accountability. Perhaps the most famous instance of this has been recounted in Julian Dibbell's *Village Voice* article (1993), "A Rape in Cyberspace or How an Evil Clown, a Haitian Trickster Spirit, Two Wizards, and a Cast of Dozens Turned a Database into a Society." Dibbell offers a harsh look at a virtual rape and the well-established community that censored and banished the self-confessed rapist, with little effect except to upset the trust of the community; when the rapist came back to the site under another name, it became clear that the designated punishment was unenforceable, because identity performance (by means of LambdaMOO's venerated gender and other aspect-swapping) allowed the culprit to perpetually and potentially infiltrate personal or social spaces. (See "Performance," this volume.) Many questions are raised and left unanswered by the LambdaMOO crisis. How is rape a gendered assault such that the victim—even when biologically male—is typically understood to be "feminized" by the aggression? And how is retribution also gendered, when, in legal or psychosocial terms, castration or other violence is considered an acceptable solution? And how is gender the social determinant for such aggression? And if actual bodies—however gendered—are unnecessary to enact or declare rape, then how might rape require redefinition as a legal, emotional, political, or cultural concept?

The Website "Babes on the Web" rehearses similar questions concerning the ways that gender is understood on- and off-line. Their homepage prominently displays an article about its inception in 1995, entitled "Sex, Identity and —." The article recounts "Babes'" early run-ins with a countersite (manned by a self-declared "proud chauvinist pig") that listed women's names and "rated" (in derogatory terms) the images of the women that appeared on "Babes." This in turn incited hurt feelings and retaliatory responses that were posted on "Babes on the Web." As the article acknowledges, the "exchange raises a number of familiar and not so familiar issues: what constitutes harassment on the Internet; the gendered nature of harassment; Web privacy; free speech and censorship; Internet service providers' responsibilities; and netiquette, or acceptable practice in electronic interaction." Further, the conflict underlines the questions concerning the ways that selves are represented and consumed on Web pages, since the women clearly did not consider their pictures standard material available for sexual objectification, even idealistically imagining that the Web by its nature resisted such in-the-flesh behavior. The article asks, if Web pages allow "the presentation of a self that exists independently of the sexed body, why, on so many women's homepages [is] the sexualized body chosen as a primary image of self?"

This is a potentially useful question to pose. First, how do we define "sexualized"? Is any depiction of a woman automatically, by definition, sexualized (or at least open to objectification and intimidating "ratings")? Second, how are women—as individuals or collectively—to understand the increasingly common practice of using likely popular names or keywords for site designations, to encourage hits from unsuspecting first-timers? For instance, in May 1999, after the Littleton, Colorado, shootings, some porn sites grabbed up the name "Columbine" to entice visitors; others regularly use celebrity names like Jennifer Love Hewitt or Foxy Brown, even when they do not feature pornographic images of the said celebrities, who are usually female or feminized, as in naked Brad Pitt pictures. The broader question, however, has to do with this vision of the Web as a means to gender-transcendence, where gender may be rendered insignificant by its performance. The experience of gender—in virtual and corporeal environments—tends to be similar, because oppressive structures and assumptions about gender remain in place.

Apprehending and Activating Gender

Allucquere Roseanne Stone has observed that attempts to transcend—or more precisely, to forget—bodies are essentially based in self-delusion. A transgender lesbian who teaches cybertheory and gender studies at the University of Texas at Austin, Stone writes, "Forgetting about the body is an old Cartesian trick, one that has unpleasant consequences for those bodies whose speech is silenced by the act of our forgetting . . . usually women and minorities" (1991: 100). Stone's focus on not forgetting—which is less a matter of remembering per se than realizing the consequences of forgetfulness, willful or not—is important to the process of apprehending gender. By apprehending, I mean comprehending or "getting" gender, or better, perceiving the ways that it gets you. To apprehend gender as a set of consequences and determinations, is to "get" the performative limitations and possibilities. The Web is a productive and provocative place for such apprehension, in large part because it provides and creates a flexible visual field, such that gender's inherent malleability (its reliance on social perceptions and expectations) is exacerbated rather than renounced.

By way of example, consider Kate Bornstein. Like Stone, Bornstein is a transgender lesbian who is exceptionally conversant with the Web as a way to get the word out, that word being that gender is a cultural—not "natural"—condition. On how to "deconstruct gender," Bornstein writes:

> The first thing to do is to ask the question: What is gender? This is a question that does not get asked; people mostly ask, "what is the difference between men and women?" They begin by presupposing a specific bi-polar gender system. The first step in taking gender apart is to ask the question; the second step is to get other people to ask the question. I think the answer is that there is no such thing as gender, other than what we say it is. (1994)

If gender is "what we say it is," then can it be unmade in the say-ing? Nice to think so, but there are preliminary questions to be con-sidered, including, who are "other people" and who are "we"? More-over, any change coming will be achieved in small steps. Bornstein says that her own understanding of gender as a convention "means I am not bound by the social constrictions of either gender. To be a man or to be a woman for me at this point in my life would be one closet or another." Avoiding such limits, such dark and confining spaces, means constant movement, a genuine and perpetual activism.

Such activism takes multiple forms and fronts, by necessity and in-genuity. Stone and Bornstein find voice and space on the Web, as do several organizations, including "women'space," which features "black women on the net"; the guerillagirl, a group of feminist artists and performers, who take up topical subjects; "cybergrrrl," the voices of women on the Web; "spiderwoman," an organization of "women who make the Web," designers and developers; "Webgrrls," activists and community organizers; and the fabulous Gender Theory site, which offers readable critiques and analyses of popular culture and other gender-troubled locations.

Each of these sites makes an argument, sets goals and horizons, and imagines new ways of regarding and countering the gender roles that too many of us take for granted. That they are able to make their cases to the potentially huge audience made available by and on the Web is a matter of exposure and potential effects, not ideology or function. The Web facilitates their activism, their ability to speak widely and persistently, but the Web does not determine their con-cerns or efforts. It only allows a particular means for activism, a means that is accessible and, at least in some cases, affordable. As Anne Balsamo (1996) argues, the body might be usefully understood as a "process," such that gender and other aspects of embodiment be-come open to question and complex understanding. The Web gives these questions and reframings a dramatic context.

Chapter 4

Race

Lisa Nakamura

> The dominance of the Web gives it the potential to re-
> form our notions of race.

What happens to race on the Web? Should we assume that anything at all "happens" to race on the Web? Proponents of cyberutopia claim the Internet is inherently democratic and color-blind because its users can engage with it anonymously; that is, users' race and gender need not be known to others when they engage in Web-chat, post texts to Websites or newsgroups, or send email. If this is true, does race even matter any more?

Indeed, the Web *can* break down the divisions which separate reader from writer, speaker from audience, self from Other. Users can enact and express their subjectivity when mouse-clicking their way through the Web; they can create individual paths through the endless series of menus and hierarchical lists which the Web offers. The vastness of the Web has contributed to the popularity of "portals" such as Excite, Alta Vista, Lycos, and others, which mediate users' experience of the Web by offering search engine assistance, news and weather reports, searchable databases, advertising, and— most of all—a friendly and familiar "front-end" to cyberspace. This chapter will discuss the ways that Web interface design, such as that evident in Web portals, reveals assumptions about users' race and ethnicity. Though the Web is a relatively new medium, it has been around long enough for its interface to have become naturalized; readers tend to focus on its content and do not sufficiently examine the political aspects of its design, or even recognize design decisions *as* political.

Internet users are often overwhelmed by the sheer mass of data on the Web. The anxiety caused by this carnivalesque riot of texts and images mirrors the unease which readers of postmodern fiction experience. Of course, the Web is much more pleasurable to use if one has a sense of order and control over the material—hence the popularity of and need for portals and their search engines. The pleasure of unbounded texts like the Web is an acquired taste, and just as the reader of new-to-postmodern fiction needs tools such as literary analysis in order to appreciate the quality of this experience, so too do Web users seek "guided readings" of the Web. This market for services which mediate the user's experience on the Web is a large and lucrative one, as the recent phenomenal success of companies such as Yahoo! and Excite has shown.

But what structures of organization mediate users' experiences with the Web, and how do these structures contribute to the ways in which race is depicted and envisioned on the Web? A close look at Web portals reveals that they are often structured in ways that reaffirm traditional racial categories rather than challenge them. Web portals condition a particular kind of reading of the Web which does not actually change its content, but rather creates a particular kind of interfaced reading, and a particular type of reader.

Portals impose order upon the enormous collection of data which is the Web by presenting the user with a series of choices, which, in the case of Excite's list of Websites about "cultures and groups," entail racial identity choices as well. When I entered the search term "race" into Excite's search field, I received a number of "hits" which were clearly about boat racing, horse racing, and so on—the kind of category shock which is an everyday occurrence on the Web. I then entered the term "racial" and was directed to a page which contained a list of clickable categories that I was encouraged to "try first." The list of ten categories read as follows:

African Diaspora
Asian American
Gay and Lesbian
Community Services
Latino Culture

Men's Issues
Native American Culture
Religion
Virtual Worlds
Women's Issues

I chose Asian American, and was presented with a series of increasingly specific categories, such as Japanese, Korean, and the like.
I noticed a few things: for example, the arrangement of this menu
only allowed me to click upon one category at a time. While my identity might encompass women's issues *and* Asian American ones *and*
Native American *and* gay and lesbian ones, all at the same time and in
more or less equal measure depending on what I was doing or how I
conceived of myself at the time, the list reified these identities and set
them up as discrete and separate from each other. In other words, it
forces the user to choose "what" they are and allows only one choice
at a time.

Far from encouraging the user's sense of a "multiple self" enabled
by this technology which Turkle (1997) celebrates in her writings, the
structure of this menu works to close off the possibility of alternate or
hybrid definitions of identity. If I attempt to read recursively by clicking on the "back" button, I can try to bring all these categories together, but the unavoidable need to choose one first still remains. Excite's structure of ranked menus and links, which seems on the face of
it to be all about choice, in fact offers little choice.

While the category "African Diaspora" does seem more nuanced
and historically grounded than "black," or "African American"
which would exclude non-Americans of African descent, this hypertextual list of identity choices reminds me of nothing more than the
National Census form, which has only recently made the category
"other" available to describe racial identity. This term has become
necessary in an increasingly multicultural and multiethnic America
where old categories for describing identity are at best misleading
and at worst inaccurate, and its existence indicates a new, less sim-
plistic and more complex understanding of race. However, Excite's
list reinforces old notions of racial identity as linked to black-and-
white definitions because it offers a limited range of choices, none of
which may reflect the identities of actual people who are using the
Web to find information about their race in particular or about "race"

in general. While this menu does not require the user to identify his or her race by clicking on a link, the experience of seeing this list reproduced from the outmoded language of demographic census taking and identity taxonomies to the Web highlights the fact that the categories of ethnicity and race are ranked as discrete from others. The list literally highlights these categories in differently colored fonts, which signify their function as branches on the decision tree of racial identity.

Excite's guided reading of race on the Web performs another interesting textual move; it lumps gender, sexual orientation, religion, and age together with race. This organizing of identity does not include "white" as a category; it is not on the menu at all. This omission is a disturbing example of the colonialist or imperialist gaze which sets up a racial Other; whiteness is defined by its absence rather than its presence. The racial category of "whiteness" is assumed to be a default option, thus creating a guided reading of the Web which assumes that its reader is white. This structure does equal disservice to whites, who are implicitly assumed not to possess a racial identity at all since the category "white" is omitted from the list, and nonwhites, whose experiences as users are invalidated and excluded.

Since "men's issues" are included in the list, as are "women's issues," it seems that gender is one of the forks in the path for reading identity on the Web. The decision to include this category acknowledges the existence of a "male identity" while excluding the possibility of a distinctively "white" one.

Very little has been published on the topic of the Web and race. While many scholars have indicated a need for further research, few have discussed the rigorous affinities between the Web as a cultural and discursive practice and the field of signifying practices that we call race. Poster's work (1995) is a notable exception: though he does not address the Web specifically in his book *The Second Media Age*, in a section entitled "Multiculturalism and the Postmodern Media Age," he points out that "as the second media age unfolds and permeates everyday practice, one political issue will be the construction of new combinations of technology with multiple genders and ethnicities" (1995:42).

His work also calls attention to the crucial element of the politics of authorship in cybernetic spaces. It is important to note that the landscape architects of the Web's forking-path structures such as portals are largely white male software engineers. Portals are highly commodified products of Silicon Valley big business; they are produced via multiple partnerships with enormously profitable multinational companies such as IBM, Microsoft, and Compaq, and as such are hardly likely to encourage the articulation of minority identities. Just as we cannot expect that popular market-driven media such as film, advertising, and television will necessarily make it a part of their mission to represent race in progressive ways—or, indeed, at all—we should not assume that Web portals will. Far from attributing the responsibility for this state of affairs to any specific individual designer or corporation, envisioning the Web as one form of popular media among others allows us to analyze our culture's limited ways of looking at race.

Like the tiny windows in submarines which are their namesake, portals offer an extremely limited and constricted view of the world. The successive series of lists they offer omit many identity choices, such as "interracial" and "white/European." This is particularly disappointing when we take into account recent predictions that the Internet would serve to level out racial inequality. Initially, hopes were high regarding the Internet's potential to produce and encourage racial equality. Zickmund (1997) writes in "Approaching the Radical Other: The Discursive Culture of Cyberhate" that the openness of the Internet "endangers the notion of a closed community" and "could become an ally in the struggle against bigotry and racism" (1997:204). This optimism is echoed in Turkle's assertion that the "more fluid sense of self" engendered by the Internet "allows a greater capacity for acknowledging diversity. It makes it easier to accept the array of our and others' inconsistent personae—perhaps with humor, perhaps with irony. We do not feel compelled to rank or judge the elements of our multiplicity. We do not feel too compelled to exclude what does not fit" (1997:261–262).

Optimistic libertarian rhetoric, such as that often seen in *Wired* magazine's editorials, is even more radical; its maxim that "information wants to be free" assumes that making information available on the Internet will liberate users from their bodies and hence from those inconvenient markers attached to the body such as racism and sexism. The equation seems simple: if nobody's body is visible while they are in cyberspace, racism and bigotry cannot exist at that time and in that place. This notion of the Web as a cure for racism is attractive. Indeed, Web features such as "chat" have enabled unique kinds of racial discourse and social interaction to occur that were impossible before, such as cross-racial role-playing in chat spaces.

Unfortunately, the Web has failed to live up to these predictions (Nakamura 1999). Far from becoming sensitized to what it feels like to be of another race in cyberspace, many users masquerading as racial minorities in chat spaces tended to depict themselves in ways that simply repeat and reenact old racial stereotypes. In many MOOs and role-playing cyberspaces one frequently comes across users masquerading as samurai and geishas, complete with swords, kimonos, and other paraphernalia lifted from older media such as film and television. This is hardly a version of ethnicity with which the contemporary Asian or Asian American user can identify, considering that neither samurai nor geisha really exist anymore. More to the point, this type of play reenacts an anachronistic version of "Asianness" which reveals more about users' fantasies and desires than it does about what it "feels like" to be Asian. (Also see "Ideology," this volume.)

Conversations about how the Web can "wipe out" race may obscure the fact that users do indeed possess bodies that are raced, bodies which are denied housing and discriminated against in job interviews, bodies which suffer institutional forms of racism off-line. Despite the various techniques the Web offers for hiding one's race, the fact that race deeply impacts most users' experiences in the world cannot be erased. This leads to another crucial aspect of race and the Web: demographics and racial representation. Does the Web look like America, to coin a phrase by President Bill Clinton? Ought it to? Does it matter? And in what ways?

Web demographics are always in flux. However, it has been known for some time that racial minorities use the Web less than do whites. Hoffman and Novak's 1998 study "Bridging the Digital Divide: The Impact of Race on Computer Access and Internet Use" states that "whites are more likely than African-Americans to have access to a computer at home and work, while African Americans are more likely to *want* access" (1998, on-line). Racial minorities have less access to the Web than do their white counterparts; they are underrepresented, partly because of the cost, both financial and cultural, of acquiring net literacy. This underrepresentation of nonwhites on-line has its roots in historical developments in American educational policy, as Jonathan Sterne (1999) describes in his essay, "The Computer

Race Meets Computer Classes: How Computers in Schools Helped Shape the Racial Topography of the Internet." Government funding to support computer instruction in public schools in the 1980s tended to favor upper-middle-class and white students, who were, ironically, likely to already possess access to computers at home. Policies such as these, which provided white students with a head start with regard to this technology, have perpetuated the vicious cycle of minority lack of access to computing in general and the Internet in particular. This situation is still playing itself out today.

Hoffman and Novak's study (1998) examines the incidence of African American *usage* of the Internet and the Web. A separate yet equally important related issue with regard to race and the Web is that of *authorship*. What are the racial demographics of those who write the content, design the interfaces, and create the search engines which make up the Web and condition our readings of it? If African Americans are underrepresented as Web users, they are even more underrepresented as Web builders.

This has serious implications for "digital culture."[1] The Web is increasingly becoming a widespread and at times unavoidable aspect of modern culture. Access to jobs, networking, and professional advancement, especially in the lucrative and quickly growing high-tech fields, often requires Web use. The continued exclusion or underrepresentation of minorities as Web builders may mean that interfaces continue to offer the same limited range of choices that are tailored, however unconsciously, to white users. Indeed, the very unconsciousness of this process makes it difficult to combat or even identify. (Young, highly educated workers at Web design companies in urban areas are, in fact, quite likely to possess sincere "liberal" views on race.) Hence, it is vital that we acquire and use theoretical tools for analyzing interface design and its unspoken biases. It is all the more important that we do this when we take into account the popularity and increasing hegemony of the Web. The dominance of the Web gives it the potential to have an immense impact on reforming our notions of race—if we can successfully increase minority participation in its design and take minorities into account as users.

The Web is the most popular incarnation of the Internet and comes the closest to constituting a "public sphere." Its accessibility and its focus on communities and community building offers unprecendentedly rich opportunities for discussion of the way identities, racial and otherwise, are being constructed and deployed. However, the Web is not yet a public sphere in a truly democratic and racially inclusive sense; demographic studies have shown that while gender and racial diversity on the Web and the Internet in general is growing, this is primarily because the Web started out and is still primarily the do- main of the white upper-middle-class male user.

However, just as this medium may result in interactions which reenact and recapitulate racist discourse and behavior, so too can the Web function to reinforce a "ranking and judging" of "multiplicity." The multiple interlacing discourses of racial identity on the Web can—as in the case of Excite's page which offers to "track down" your race and ethnicity if you plug in your last name into its search field— as easily serve to reinforce biological and essentialist notions of race as they can deconstruct and challenge them.

The Web has come to stand for the Internet in the minds of most users; practically speaking, the Web *is* cyberspace. The Web is that most elastic and thus far most hardy of electronic media forms: het- eroglossic, multigeneric, channeled, and polymorphous. Like the novel as characterized by Mikhail Bakhtin (1981), it has successfully assimilated and incorporated other cybergenres such as chat, Java ap- plets, email, and so on, and is successfully subsuming them into it- self. As Web browser applications become even more fully featured, users need never leave the Web in order to write and read email, download files, listen to music, and chat.

In addition, the Web has the aura of truth. I often describe it to oth- ers as a garage sale of information—that is, while you will always find something, the value, accuracy, and relevance of what you find may be doubtful. Scholars and students need to be especially cautious when using the Web, more so than they would while scanning, say, the *MLA Bibliography*. This precaution is particularly advised since the Web's in- formation comes to us in slick, telegenic, attractive images and text which give the impression of authenticity and legitimacy and therefore seem true. All this data comes to us on the same desktop—out of the same pipe, so to speak—and represents legitimate scholarship as well as assorted data ranging from misinformation at best to crackpot theo- ries at worst, as all somehow equal to each other.

Leading sites of information are often delivered in the glossy, de- ceiving guise of a "legitimate" homepage—and, as we know, they can also contain racist or hate speech. There are numerous examples of this phenomenon: recently when I plugged the search term "Holocaust" into a search engine, I was directed to a neo-Nazi Website which made the case that the Holocaust never happened, as well as sites such as the "American Holocaust Memorial—a memorial to the holocaust of abortion and its correlations with the Nazi holocaust."

As this particular example shows, the Web is indeed a place where race "happens" and is constructed not only through the content of the texts on the Internet, but also by specific and particular forms of electronic linkage, ranked menus, search engines, and other forms of mediation which guide our readings of them. In this example—the linkage by hypertext of the Holocaust to militant antichoice groups—race "happens" with gender in ways that are visible and striking, as they could not in other media. And what is more, race happens on the Web in ways unique to the medium of hypertext, ways that illustrate both its ability to challenge notions of canonized or linear racial and "other" histories and identities, and ways which may force particular racialized identity choices on the part of the user.

Gloria Anzaldúa is not generally cited as a source in essays on technology, perhaps because her work tends not to address the issue head on. On the other hand, Anzaldúa's critical vocabulary, her take on multiculturalism and the cultural means by which fragmentary "mestiza" or racially and culturally mixed selves are articulated, marginalized, and created, are extremely useful when one is describing the ways in which recursive, resistant readings of portaled hypertexts can be tracked. She provides a model of resistant reading which challenges racism, and most importantly demonstrates the ways in which reading and writing, on the Web or otherwise, can become revolutionary acts.

In *Borderlands/La Frontera*, Anzaldúa (1987) has written her own search engine for racial and gender identity. In her work, she continually invokes and clicks through search terms such as "white," "colored," "queer," "race," and so on, creating her own kind of multicultural hypertext, one which allows these terms to exist in webbed relation to each other, and to come together in the figure of the new mestiza. The mestiza has a "webbed" consciousness. Her mission is to "take inventory. . . . Just what did she inherit from her ancestors? This weight on her back—which is the baggage from the Indian mother, which the baggage from the Spanish father, which the baggage from the Anglo?" (1987:82). As the mestiza clicks her way through the various, divergent paths of identity, one can envision her working through the "Excite" list, clicking every keyword and searchpath. The mestiza on the Web "reinterprets history and, using new symbols, she shapes new myths. She adopts new perspectives towards the darkskinned, women, and queers. She strengthens her tolerance (and intolerance) for ambiguity" (1997:82).

Indeed, Web portals function in a similarly dual way; they encourage tolerance by acknowledging "diverse" identities, yet create ambiguities about identities which fall between the cracks of hierarchical lists, those sites or non-spaces of hybrid being which seem to hover phantasmatically between the fine strands of the portaled Web. What if you just do not fit into any of the categories available on the list, or do not consider any one of them "dominant" but are nonetheless required by the interface to choose one first?

Anzaldúa's manifesto "La Consciencia de la Mestiza: Towards a New Consciousness" was written in 1987 and thus predates the Web by several years. However, it also functions as a portal. Her book is a portal which debunks the notion that one must necessarily choose one racial, gender, or ethnic identity. It seeks to permit an infinitely clickable interface to culture: the mestiza, "like others having or living in more than one culture . . . get[s] multiple, often opposing messages. The coming together of two self-consistent but habitually incompatible frames of reference causes *un choque*, a cultural collision" (1987:78). This "shock" has a political valence, as does the experience of Web users whose encounters with portals of ethnicity forces them to take paths which lead to stereotyped and limited destinations. Like the Web itself, Anzaldúa's text fails to come to solid conclusions about these terms and the search remains open-ended. Her guided reading is like an ideal notion of hypertext; it is an interface where taxonomic lists and nested menus of terms blur and converge. Also like the Web, hers is a diverse and multigeneric text, incorporating poetry, different languages, varied forms of address, and revisionist history.

As Web portals and other guided readings and forms of mediation come to characterize the Web and become widely used and in some cases indispensable—and thus hegemonic and dominant—means of navigating it, it is all the more important that we become sensitive to the ways that these mediations categorize racial and gender identity. When the new mestiza on the Web grasps her mouse and starts clicking, she reads in a participatory way rather than a passive one. She surfs back and forth through the garage sale that is cyberspace, never settling with just one category on the list, but always moving to the next and the next. She builds reading webs between them and performs the vital work of resistant reading on the Web. However, as portals become commercialized, corporate interfaces and flashily franchised front ends to cyberspace, this work becomes more and more difficult, requiring immense effort to work and read against the grain.

Of course, economic, educational, and cultural inequities amplify the mestiza's difficulties in cyberspace; she is less likely to learn the back doors around portals when her access to networked computers is so limited. The "newbie mestiza," using the Web for the first time, is more likely to take Excite's suggestions to "start here," and to allow her reading to be guided by an "easy-to-use" portal which subjects her to its particular hierarchies about race. New users are particularly vulnerable to the ideologies hidden in portals, since successful on-line services such as America Online have thrived primarily by targeting their products toward inexperienced users who identify themselves as "non-computer people." As Hoffman and Novak note, African Americans are more likely than whites to identify themselves in this way and thus to rely on a portaled on-line service rather than an Internet service provider, as their only means of Internet access from the home.

Ultimately, the question of race and its relation to the World Wide Web boils down to the need for expanded minority access and representation on-line. More racial minorities need to write and put up their own webs, webs in which a mestiza or "other" consciousness can become part of the grain, rather than always working against it. Websites such as NetNoir and Latino Link do open up spaces for nonwhite users—perhaps most importantly, they foreground racial identity in ways that the vast majority of other commercial Websites neglect altogether. These and other racial and ethnic identity Websites, many of them created by individuals without corporate affiliations who put up "zines" and other alternative publications expressing their ethnic and racial identities, productively challenge the false but popular and sentimentally utopian notion of cyberspace as "race-free." However, the limitations of the Web's powers as a force against bigotry and racism are considerable. Until increased education, economic parity, and changing cultural priorities make the Web accessible to more racial minorities, the medium will reflect the often unconscious racial assumptions and priorities of corporate America. In the meantime the Web has yet to live up to its promise of truly blurring the lines between reader and writer, speaker and audience, self and Other. We must continue to be aware of and question what is missing from the various menus offered us on the Web and work to rewrite these menus in ways that include all of us.

NOTES

Parts of this chapter were originally delivered as a paper at the 1998 American Studies Association conference. Thanks go to Randy Bass at Georgetown for presiding over the panel and providing the inspiration (and invitation) for me to produce this work. Additional thanks to Sonoma State University's English department and Arts and Humanities Division for travel and research support.

1. I put this term in quotes partly to acknowledge its overuse as a cliché, but also to point out its status as a misnomer; while we tend to think of culture as rich, varied, layered, and possessing depth, digital culture as envisioned by popular media and as represented by corporate portals is strikingly consistent as to look-and-feel. In other words, it tends to be flat, generic, and undiverse. Indeed, digital culture as it exists today is monocultural, clearly not "multicultural."

Chapter 5

Political Economy

Vincent Mosco

We stand at the brink of another revolution. This one
will involve unprecedentedly inexpensive communication; all the computers will join together to communicate with us and for us. Interconnected globally, they
will form a network, which is being called the information highway. A direct precursor is the present Internet, which is a group of computers joined and exchanging information using current technology.

—Bill Gates 1995:3–4

These words by Bill Gates, the enormously successful president of the
Microsoft Corporation, give us more than just a definition of the
World Wide Web. They announce a vision of a world transformed by
computer communication. This chapter takes up the vision that Gates
and others have promised and evaluates it against what we know
about the World Wide Web, particularly in its political and economic
dimensions. In order to do this effectively we need to start with an
overview of a political-economic perspective.

What Is Political Economy?

Two definitions of political economy capture the wide range of specific and general angles to the approach. In the narrow sense, political
economy is *the study of the social relations, particularly the power relations,
that mutually constitute the production, distribution, and consumption of*

resources, including communication resources. From this perspective, political economy studies power or the ability to get what you want even when others don't want you to get it. This perspective raises the following questions: Who has power in the media and communication business? How does power work in the world of cyberspace? Another way of describing political economy is to broaden this meaning, focusing on a set of central qualities that characterize the approach. These include social transformation or history, the social totality, moral philosophy, and praxis or social action.

Political economy has consistently placed the goal of understanding social change and historical transformation in the foreground. For eighteenth-century political economists such as Adam Smith, this meant comprehending the great capitalist revolution, the vast social upheaval that would transform societies based primarily on agricultural labor into commercial, manufacturing, and, eventually, industrial societies. For their nineteenth-century counterparts like Karl Marx, it meant examining the dynamic forces within capitalism and between it and other forms of political-economic organization, in order to understand the processes of social change that would, ultimately, transform capitalism into socialism. Today's mainstream discipline of economics, which began to coalesce against political economy in the late nineteenth century, tends to set aside this concern for the dynamics of history and social change in order to turn political economy into the science of economics, whose lawlike statements are constructed to fit static, rather than dynamic, social conditions. Contemporary political economists, however, occupying various positions distinct from what has become economic orthodoxy, continue the tradition of studying social transformation.

Political economy is also characterized by an interest in examining the social whole or the totality of social relations that constitute the economic, political, social, and cultural fields. From the time of Adam Smith, whose interest in understanding social life was not constrained by disciplinary boundaries, through Karl Marx and on to contemporary theorists, political economy has consistently aimed to build on the unity of the political and the economic by accounting for their mutual constitution and for their relationship to wider social and cultural spheres of activity.

Political economy is noted for its commitment to moral philosophy, understood as both an interest in the values that help to constitute social behavior and in those moral principles that ought to guide efforts to change it. For Adam Smith, this meant understanding values like acquisitiveness and individual freedom that were contributing to the rise of commercial capitalism. For Marx , however, moral philosophy meant the ongoing struggle between the drive to realize self and social value in human labor and the drive to reduce labor to a marketable commodity. The moral philosophy of contemporary political economy tends to emphasize democracy or the fullest possible public participation in the decisions that affect our lives.

Following from this view, social praxis, or the fundamental unity of thinking and action, also occupies a central place in political economy. Specifically, against orthodox positions which separate the sphere of research from social intervention, political economists have consistently viewed intellectual life as a form of social transformation and social intervention as a form of knowledge. Although they differ fundamentally on what should characterize intervention—ranging from Thomas Malthus who supported open sewers as a form of population control to Marx, who called on labor to realize itself in revolution—political economists are united in the view that the division between research and action is artificial and must be overturned. Today, political economists interested in the Web work to promote universal access and full participation in the Information Society.

The Political Economy of the Web

This section applies a political economy perspective to the development of communication and information technologies, particularly to the Web. In 1844, Samuel Morse and Stephen Vail exchanged the first message by telegraph. Advances in communication and information technology have taken us a long way in a relatively short time. For example, according to a U.S. Commerce Department study released in November 1997, the computing and telecommunications industries grew by 57 percent during the 1990s to $866 billion, making it the nation's largest industry ahead of construction, food products, and automotive manufacturing. But the many technological changes should not lead us to miss the institutional pattern established by the telegraph, which has pervaded subsequent technologies, including the telephone, radio, television, and now the computer.

The pattern started with competition among inventors, but this evaporated with the rapid growth of monopoly corporate control, which was opposed by a citizens' movement that forced government and business to pay at least token attention to fairness and equity, in addition to profit and market share. As the economic historian Richard DuBoff (1984) concluded:

> Virtually all subsequent developments in telecommunications, can be seen, in latent form, in the conversion of telegraph technology into a commodity bought and sold for profit and saved from the "wastes of competition" by the collective actions that preserved monopoly prerogatives within the industry and shielded their beneficiaries from public accountability. (1984:53–54)

DuBoff's research demonstrates that it took just twenty years from the commercial birth of the telegraph industry for the fierce competition over Morse's "lightning wires" to result in the monopoly control of the Western Union Telegraphy Company. Successful monopolies master a range of strategies, economic and political, offensive and defensive. Western Union was particularly good at manipulating prices and stock offerings to drive out and swallow up its competition. The lessons were not lost on companies that aspired to similar market dominance over subsequent communication and information technologies. AT&T used price fixing to weaken and then buy out the competition, forging a nearly impregnable wall around its telephone monopoly for over half a century. RCA, born out of the patent sharing agreements among the oligopoly of AT&T, General Electric, and Westinghouse, dominated broadcasting for nearly as long. RCA was so strong in AM radio in the late 1940s that the U.S. government agreed to move the entire channel allocation it had given to the technically superior but fledgling FM service, thereby making 400,000 FM receivers obsolete. This government action eventuated in the RCA buyout (at bargain basement prices) of many desperate FM stations.

So it should come as no surprise today that the icon for innovative Information Age companies, Microsoft, is using an operating system that it took from Apple (whose software people got it from Xerox) to drive out the competition in a wide range of information products and services, including the fundamental gateway to cyberspace, the desktop. As U.S. government court documents now reveal, Microsoft has tried to force major computer makers like Compaq to put the Microsoft Explorer Web browser on the desktop of each Compaq PC, rather than that of competitors like Netscape, the company responsible for this innovation in the first place, or risk losing its license to the Windows operating system. Cyber guru Steven Johnson (1997) describes this in the *New York Times*: "Imagine that Microsoft controls the market for office desks, and it is also a major telephone maker. One day it announces that all its desks will come with built-in phones—thereby putting all the other phone manufacturers out of business" (1997:A-27).

Of course, Compaq itself is part of a growing concentration in the computer hardware business. By the end of 2001, four computer makers will control half the overall PC market, up from 24 percent of the market in 1998, according to a report by Charles Wolf, PC analyst for Credit Suisse First Boston.

Microsoft is out to trump AT&T more than metaphorically because it is not only mimicking the historic monopolist in using innovation to gain an unfair competitive advantage, but it is also taking innovations developed elsewhere (Apple, Netscape), changing them slightly, and using them to seize control over strategic access points, such as the computer operating system to consolidate its monopoly power. It is more than ironic that Microsoft is using what amounts to the same justification that AT&T got away with for half a century to sanction its monopoly. AT&T argued that its long-distance monopoly was a natural extension of its local service monopoly and an end to the former would undermine the latter and therefore the universality of the system. Microsoft now maintains that the integrity of the network and universal access to cyberspace require seamless control; whoever controls the operating system must control extensions to it, including the keys that unlock the gate to cyberspace. It took fifty years to end the AT&T monopoly and now we face a new and perhaps more formidable one.

Microsoft's operating system runs 90 percent of the computers in the world. It has made significant investments across every segment of the information and entertainment industries, including publishing, video imaging, and cable television; essentially wherever there is potential competition, it is buying up, joining with, and otherwise turning itself into the dark side of that Information Age euphemism "convergence." Indeed, Microsoft is the millennium's icon for the convergent monopoly. In addition to its threat to stop licensing

Windows software to Compaq, Microsoft stands accused of a pattern of applying monopoly power against companies large and small. For example, when the giant manufacturer of microprocessors, Intel, began developing its own Internet software, Microsoft complained and forced Intel, a long-time partner of Microsoft, to back off. After Spyglass, Inc. started supplying Microsoft its early browser technology, Microsoft announced that it would give it away free. This meant that Spyglass, which had licensed the software to other firms, immediately lost its major source of revenue. In another case, Microsoft struck a deal with one of its primary Internet competitors, America Online. If the latter agreed to use Microsoft's Web browser as the primary one for its millions of subscribers, Microsoft would give America Online prime space on the desktop of all personal computers using Windows software. Venture capitalists on the lookout for potentially lucrative start-up firms regularly meet privately with Microsoft executives to learn about the company's plans to extend its convergent monopoly. Why? As one venture capitalist put it, to "stay out of the way of the steamroller" (Lohr and Markoff 1998).

Numerous myths make it particularly difficult to think clearly about this problem. Indeed their growth prompts me to declare a corollary to Moore's Law, the loose observation frequently cited by technophiles to the effect that the processing power of the computer doubles every eighteen months. The corollary is Gore's Law, named after the American Vice President and originator of the noble myth of the Global Information Infrastructure. Gore's Law states that myths about the Information Society double in their distance from reality every eighteen months. One of today's leading cyber myths trumpets the wonders of *convergence* which refers to several things, including the technical convergence of systems seamlessly linked by common standards and a common digital language. It also refers to the breakdown of industry barriers that once separated print from broadcasting from telecommunication as firms converge in a vast and lucrative electronic services arena. But the myth of convergence glosses over the ways it enables Microsoft and other convergent monopolies to extend their power by occupying and policing central nodes in the key networks of production, distribution, and exchange in the information economy.

The power of myth to deny history makes it difficult to think that the problems of another era—like the tendency of big companies to dominate an industry, setting the terms for prices, product, and labor—are of any consequence today. Yet, the web of connections linking just a handful of companies—Microsoft, Disney/ABC, Time Warner-Turner, GE/NBC, AT&T-TCI, CBS-Viacom, MCI-Worldcom, and the News Corp—arguably now shapes almost every major sector of the Information Age, including cable television, TV and film production, wired and wireless telephone, Internet technology and content, home video and games, sports teams satellites, newspapers, magazines, books, television broadcasting, music and recording, and theme parks.

What Is the Web? Where Did It Come From?

The World Wide Web is more than just a network of computer communication technologies. The specific characteristics of the Web result from the particular way it has developed. That is why a political economy perspective considers it crucially important to learn about the history of the Web, its relationship to the history of similar technologies, and how the Web is influenced by trends in business, government, and in society and culture.

The Web grew out of the convergence of computer and communication technologies which began at the end of World War II. In fact, the computer developed during the war to enhance the effectiveness of automatic weapons. In the 1950s almost all the funding for computer research came from the U.S. military, which gave large contracts to commercial firms like IBM and AT&T. In turn, these companies sold the first computer systems, including the first networks that linked them to telephone lines, to the U.S. Defense Department. Between 1958 and 1974 the U.S. military bought 35 to 50 percent of all computer circuits. By providing a major market for these products, the U.S. military was able to influence the development of computers and to provide the industry with the funding that kept it alive. So dependent was the electronics industry on military contracts that in 1957 the prominent American business magazine *Fortune* worried about the future of the computer if the Cold War were to end: "Peace, if it came suddenly, would hit the industry very hard" (Harris 1957:216). In 1958 the military agency responsible for developing computing technology created the very first example of the World

Wide Web, Arpanet (for Advanced Research Projects Network), which was made up of computers that connected military researchers and their commercial contractors by phone lines.

The Web therefore did not originate, as popular myths maintain, in the work of amateur tinkerers toying with new technologies in their home workshops. Rather, it began out of the need to bring together military researchers and their industrial partners who were responsible for the major arms buildup in the West from the 1960s through the 1980s. True, the personal computer arose in part from the work of a few brilliant young amateurs. But by the time Steve Jobs was creating the first Apple computer and Bill Gates was selling his first operating system software to run the IBM PC, computer networks were an established tool in Western military and business operations.

This early history is important for understanding the contemporary Web because it helped to establish the intense interest in putting business and military security interests first. This meant that networks were under tight corporate or government security control, run on the authoritarian principle of centralized management of the network, with little opportunity for people to freely use these networks for anything more than established rules permitted. One commercial example of this principle was the Dialog network which was set up by the major military contractors General Electric and Lockheed. Dialog permitted subscribers to dial up a database to search for information for which they would pay a subscription fee and a charge for the amount of time spent on the system. Subscribers could not send information or communicate with one another; they paid to search available stores of information.

Nevertheless, even as the military and business were perfecting forerunners of the Internet, individual engineers, university researchers, and people interested in exploring the democratic uses of technology were trying out the potential for connecting the new stand-alone personal computers through telephone lines. By the mid-1980s, the first of what we would today call electronic bulletin boards had sprung up to use computers for unrestricted communication, ranging from just chatting and playing games to mobilizing citizen groups for political action. The WELL, a network of California computer enthusiasts, was one of the first, and on a much larger scale, Peacenet was established in the mid-1980s as a nonprofit network that by 1987 connected 2,500 subscribers and 300 organizations in 70 countries to advance communication among citizen activists. It provided some of the first public email, bulletin board, computer conferencing, and data research services for activists around the world, including the earliest links between people working for democratic social change across what was then the great divide between the Soviet Union and the United States and its allies.

By the time the Web arrived, the pattern was set between a dominant centralized group of networks based on the model of ability to pay with careful security controls that limited communication, and another set of networks that were more open, democratic, and committed to the widest possible flows of communication. This pattern continues today. The dominant model includes large corporations, such as America Online, Microsoft, and the major telephone companies, providing Internet services for a monthly or hourly fee. It also features software providers like Microsoft and Netscape using their browser programs to direct users to selections offered by other large businesses, including media conglomerates such as Time-Warner, which rely on extensive advertising and have financial deals with these software providers. Another variation on the dominant model is a handful of data service providers, such as Lexis-Nexis, the oldest of them all, and a subsidiary of the giant publishing firm Reed-Elsevier. For a very high per usage fee Lexis-Nexis provides businesses with immediate access to an archived database of the world's newspapers, business publications, government reports, and a variety of other material.

The alternative pattern lives on in community networks, mainly called Freenets, which rely on community support to provide free access to the Web through terminals located in public schools, libraries, and post offices, in addition to free home access. It also lives on in the tens of thousands of individual and community "publishers" who develop homepages and special interest bulletin boards and chatrooms that encourage a freer and more broadly based exchange of information.

The costs of building and expanding the Web have become an increasingly important issue because thus far governments have paid for much of this either directly through budget allocations to research and development, or indirectly by funding universities or subsidizing Web-related companies. However, government support is declining because governments have cut budgets and because

"With the Web still in its early years, there is a lot of experimentation with alternative ways to use the Web for profit." buy.com site. http://buy.com

many believe that the private marketplace should sustain the Web. Although governments are still providing help to construct the Web, support research to improve it, and help those who cannot afford access, even these activities are coming under considerable criticism from those who feel that government should not intervene in what are believed to be private marketplace decisions, and from those who wonder about the wisdom of building computer networks when governments are cutting back on essential services like food and health care to the poor. As a result, alternative means of funding the Web have grown and are likely to have a significant impact on its development.

The means of funding media was not always obvious to investors and, when chosen, was not always approved by audiences. For example, when radio broadcasting came along, many people felt that a device that could bring news and entertainment directly into the home was too powerful to permit private developers to control. Thus, many countries, such as Britain, for example, maintained complete government authority over radio. Other countries with a weaker tradition of government control, like the United States, experimented with various forms of funding until a few private broadcasters hit on commercial advertising as the best means of making money. But many Americans reacted angrily against commercial messages because it was considered inappropriate to sell products directly in people's living rooms at all hours of the day. The government was forced to step in and regulate the hours of advertising (mainly to daytime hours during the week). Regulations were loosened in the 1930s, after commercial radio had been on the air for over ten years.

We have become so used to advertising in the mass media that there is nothing like the resistance to radio advertising when companies begin turning to Internet advertising as a way to make money. Nevertheless, with the Web still in its early years, there is a lot of experimentation with alternative ways to use the Web for profit. Many companies, including some of the largest like Microsoft, invested heavily in developing Web newspapers, magazines, games, and other entertainment that they hoped to sell directly to subscribers. The view was that if people pay for the daily newspaper, they would also pay for a paper or magazine regularly delivered to their homes electronically. As it turns out, people are very reluctant to pay for information on the Web, particularly if there are free print and electronic alternatives. Almost every venture in this area has failed and most companies provide news and information on the Web without charge and make money by selling advertising and by using their Web-based media as a good advertisement for their print editions. Time-Warner uses its Pathfinder Website to sell advertising and to promote its magazines, films, cable television channels, and other media products. Web-based games and entertainment have met a similar fate. Although it is premature to conclude that people will not pay for Web information and entertainment, a mass market is not likely to develop in this area for some time.

The other major alternative for commercializing the Web is through the sale of products, or "e-commerce" as it is widely known. Today, supporters of turning the Web into an electronic shopping mall like to say that you can buy just about anything on the Web. Anyone who has surfed the Web would have to agree that it is possible to use a credit card or telephone to buy anything from the standard products you would find in a department store, shop, or printed catalog to, say, less legitimate products and services, including pornography, weapons, and gambling. Yet because people are reluctant to trust Web companies with sensitive information like a credit card number, or because they would rather go to a shop to look at a product before making a purchase, the Web has not become a site for mass consumption. Although e-commerce is growing, it remains a small proportion of retail sales. Nevertheless, many of the major Web companies are investing heavily in e-commerce in the hope of taking a large chunk of the market from traditional retailers. Microsoft, for example, is joining up with companies knowledgeable in specific markets to provide travel, ticket purchasing, music CDs, videos, and other retail goods. New companies like Amazon.com hope to become major booksellers simply by taking Web orders for a list of several million titles. Governments are providing help by holding off on enforcing sales tax statutes for Web purchases. In the meantime, advertising increasingly fills the Web pages of companies large and small, as well as those of individual homepages. Commercialization is perhaps the most important trend on the Web and many of the new Web start-up companies based in high-tech districts like Manhattan's "Silicon Alley" have found they cannot remain in business unless they fundamentally shift their work to produce new and innovative forms of electronic advertising.

Businesses are increasingly interested in using the Web to sell more than products and services. They see enormous opportunities for profit in selling information about the people who purchase or even just come into a shop to browse. Information about visits to a site, measured in clicks or actual purchases, is sought after by companies that use this information to advertise more efficiently to people with specific interests. Although this is a major motivation to gather detailed information on how people are using the Web, it is not the only one. Governments, particularly the police and other security authorities, are interested in using Web data to develop background information on citizens to determine their possible connection to criminal activities, to further intelligence investigations, and to make connections between people and their activities. There is nothing fundamentally different between this activity and more traditional forms of wiretapping and surveillance, except that the Web provides a more powerful form of surveillance than any previous technology.

There are enormous economic and governmental incentives to intrude on and violate people's basic right to privacy on the Web. This interest in using the Web to learn about and control people's behavior, however, clashed with the business need to provide people with privacy guarantees in order to encourage them to feel comfortable enough to shop on the Web. As long as companies are unable to guarantee security, including security from intruding hackers, people will be reluctant to shop at the electronic mall. Efforts to provide a software solution have failed because of the technical difficulties of guaranteeing against hacking and because of the clash of basic interests. Governments, particularly that of the United States, do not want to approve of highly sophisticated security or encryption software because they want to retain the right to tap into the Web for what they believe are legitimate police activities.

Although the resolution of the privacy issue will have an important bearing on future Web use, it is likely that more and more of our daily routine will require a growing amount of Web activity. This is a significant problem, because the vast majority of the world's people, including a majority of people in the industrialized world, do not have access to the Web. As for people in the less developed world, where even the telephone remains a luxury, the likelihood that Web access will be made available to anyone other than the richest people in major cities is remote. Although access is more widespread in industrialized nations, it remains concentrated among the wealthiest in society (as does access to all other electronic media) and among university populations, whose access is subsidized. For most people, the cost of hardware, software, and access fees is well beyond their budgets. Although this was a problem with earlier technologies like the telephone and broadcasting, access bottlenecks were eased because the government's commitment to public service balanced the tendencies of the market to concentrate access among the rich. This is no longer the case. Except for a handful of government programs that provide little more than media publicity, people have to pay their own way to ride the Web.

The absence of government involvement has consequences beyond the ability to afford Web access. The lack of educational programs to teach people how to use the Web effectively and the dearth of access sites in public places like post offices, community centers, or government facilities make it more difficult for people to develop their Web capabilities. Consequently, even if governments changed policies and expanded the subsidized distribution of hardware and software, or provided support for low-cost access freenets or community nets, the lack of training would leave a major bottleneck. This means that as more and more information is transferred to the Web, including everything from consumer, school, and community information, those who cannot afford access or lack access skills will be at a distinct disadvantage.

In the early days of the Web, commentators felt that with its ease of electronic mail connections and opportunities for people to offer their views on politics and the issues of the day, the Web would enrich our sense of community and of citizenship. The growth of community-based freenets certainly added to the talk about virtual electronic communities. (See "Community," this volume.) However, the expanding commercialization of the Web, the packaging of content to look like television programming, and the expansion of pay services over freenets, have raised the concern that the Web is turning out to be just another medium whose major providers are interested in expanded markets rather than building communities and more focused on building a base of consumers than in producing better citizens. Nevertheless, there remain strong groups of people for whom the idea of building local and global communities through the Web continues to be a major goal. One can certainly find a wide variety of such communities based largely on interest in a spectrum of political issues from the rights of women and labor to the advocacy of religious fundamentalism. These groups may very well be defining a new form of citizenship—one that is either too large for the nation-state because it encompasses people worldwide, or too narrow for the nation-state because its aim is to enrich a local community. We are observing elements of an effort to replace what appears to be a declining identification with the nation-state with genuine alternatives facilitated by electronic connections. The global electronic links forged by the Zapatista rebels in the Mexican province of Chiapas beginning in 1996 provided a remarkable window into this new possibility. Nevertheless, it remains questionable whether groups will use the Web to exercise new forms of citizenship and build new forms of community when the pressures mount to make the Web a global shopping mall.

Chapter 6

Cyberspace

Rob Shields

Cyberspace is a metaphor.

Cyberspace and Other Self-Fulfilling Prophecies

I was tempted to begin this chapter with the question, "What is cyberspace?" However, this immediately puts us on the wrong track. Why? Consider the following scene: You are playing a guessing game such as "20-Questions." You begin by giving a hint as to whether you are thinking of an animal, a vegetable, or a mineral. Or perhaps a thing or a person. But what hint do you give if you are thinking of cyberspace? None of the categories really fit. You are, after all, thinkng of computer code, of bits and bytes—of 100111100010110001 (cf. Negroponte 1998). So the first answer to the question "What is cyberspace?" is a paradox like a Zen kaon: "Cyberspace is something else."

Of course, cyberspace is not a void. But neither is it like geographical space—it does not "contain" places. In fact it does not contain anything at all. Instead, cyberspace is a metaphor that conjures up an image or an idea of the potential of information and telecommunication networks which are formed by computers linked by telecommunications (such as telephone exchanges, fiber-optic cables, or wireless signals). If anything, it is these computers and the files stored in their memory banks and on digital media that should be thought of as the "places" and "things" in cyberspace, with cyberspace itself something that is imagined only because the network has become so dense and so all-pervasive that it is as if another, invisible, plane of reality had been created.

Cyberspace is a self-fulfilling prophecy, slowly coming into existence as more and more computers are "wired" to the Internet. The Web appears in writings on cyberspace like an "ether" of computer-mediated communications (cf. Sardar and Ravetz 1996) which only becomes apparent as more and more computers are linked by more and more connections so that more and more information is exchanged every minute. Here is a typical definition of cyberspace:

> Q. So just what is cyberspace?
>
> A. More ecosystem than machine, cyberspace is a bioelectronic environment that is literally universal: It exists everywhere there are telephone wires, coaxial cables, fiber-optic lines or electromagnetic waves.
>
> This environment is "inhabited" by knowledge, including incorrect ideas, existing in electronic form. It is connected to the physical environment by portals which allow people to see what's inside, to put knowledge in, to alter it, and to take knowledge out. Some of these portals are one-way (e.g. television receivers and television transmitters); others are two-way (e.g. telephones, computer modems). (Nunes 1995)

This kind of understanding of cyberspace is shared by many, including two well-known figures involved with the Electronic Frontier Foundation, Mitch Kapor and John Perry Barlow (see Gans and Goffman 1990), who call cyberspace "the place you are when you are on the telephone." But the grammatical mistake—perhaps made on purpose—equates self and place together as "the place you are." This suggests that such definitions do not fully capture users' feelings that they are not only in an environment and interacting with objects and people in an environment, but that they are also in some way *transported* and *transformed* by cyberspace.

Michael Benedikt (1992) was one of the first academic writers to describe cyberspace, calling it "a new universe, a parallel universe created and sustained by the world's computers and communication lines." It is a place, "entered equally from a basement in Vancouver, a boat in Port-au-Prince, a cab in New York, a garage in Texas City, an apartment in Rome, an office in Hong Kong, a bar in Kyoto, a café in Kinshasa, a laboratory on the Moon" (1992:1). Some have envisioned cyberspace less as an information domain and more literally as an environment—an extension of the idea of computer-generated virtual environments. For a time, "virtual environments" and "virtual space" came to replace "cyberspace" in the popular media. However, the terms refer to very different spatial *scales*: virtual environments are human-scaled while cyberspace(s) are imagined as city-sized or even global. Therefore, the term "cyberspace" works best as a means of describing the global interconnection of computers.

The idea that cyberspace may be a distinct plane of reality or a "different world" gives rise to arcane debates about how it is connected to the face-to-face spaces of everyday life. Much of the early literature treated the Net as an autonomous zone, free of the constraints and realpolitik of the spaces of bodies and territorial ambitions. (See "Community," this volume.) The commercial underpinnings—such as the software necessary to connect to the Net and its military origins—were neglected in this approach. Cyberspace was treated as a utopian zone, an escape from the everyday, from the body ("the meat"), and from the compromises of life in the sorts of advanced industrial societies that could produce such sophisticated telecommunications. The liminal (*limen*, threshold) has always been an opportunity for new visions of society, and cyberspace is often depicted as:

> a new totality, an "open ended universality" (as Levy states it) in which cyberspace "exemplifies the simultaneous, horizontal, purely spatial form of transmission." It is, Levy concludes his report: "with its teeming, swarming communities, the budding, branching intergrowth of its works, as if every memory of all mankind had expanded in a single instant, in a vast act of simultaneous collective intelligence, converging towards the present in a silent flash of light, neurones [sic] as the comets to burn forever bright." Sorely quixotic and absurd, this sort of deification can hardly find a rationale EVEN in the most zealous ad campaign, no less a report on the state of cyberspace. But the global mind, the open-ended totality, the society of mind, the cyborg body are linked by illusions whose "utopias" are a cross between conjecture and desire. (Druckrey n.d.)

Despite this, one on-line source comments: "For literally millions of 'netters,' cyberspace is a real place with real potentials—and it is precisely this blurring of the real and the unreal which marks Baudrillard's postmodern moment of the hyperreal. From this perspective, the compelling image of 'Internet as world' pushes us beyond the world, beyond its containment" (Nunes 1995). What does it mean to discover a new world? Cyberspace breaks the closure of the known world—a geographic totality which has been largely closed since 1492 when Columbus discovered the "New World" (Todorov 1984:13–14). Cyberspace signals a concept which attempts to create a totality of which and in which humans are the absolute masters.

Consensual Hallucination

As other writers in this volume have noted, the word "cyberspace" has its origins in Canadian novelist William Gibson's book *Neuromancer* (1984). In it, cyberspace is first described as something like flying over a vast city lit up at night. Rather than buildings, however, litup geometric shapes—cubes, pyramids, and boxes—symbolize the large computer databanks of major corporations. There is little mention of individuals' personal computers—they scarcely existed when the book was written. In fact, the first widely available IBM desktop PC only became available in 1980, and using telephone modems to connect one's home computer to local databases and information exchanges (bulletin board services or BBSs) only became popular around 1985.

> Cyberspace - A consensual hallucination experienced daily by billions of legitimate operators, in every nation. . . . A graphic representation of data abstracted from the banks of every computer in the human system. Unthinkable complexity. Lines of light ranged in the nonspace of the mind, clusters and constellations of data. Like city lights, receding. (Gibson 1984:51)

From this imagining of what networked computers were to become, we might conclude that Gibson was wrong in that he foresaw this network as primarily corporate. Private citizens entered only as poachers via some sort of brain implant which gave them the feeling of perceiving cyberspace through all their senses and above all through the tactile relationship of their mobile body (or a representation of it) with larger, stationary geometric forms which were temples of corporate data and information. In *Neuromancer*, the challenge is to enter these databanks and give the information in them to other corporations.

Cyberspace City

In Gibson's vision, there is thus a politics to cyberspace—and the form of redistributive justice in the book's plot is a David and Goliath struggle between disenfranchised individuals and corporate holders of power. This romantic vision proved extremely powerful in shaping the imaginations of computer programmers and entrepreneurs in the early 1990s. They envisioned either a total body immersion experience in cyberspace; an avatar (a game piece or animated cartoon character that represented the user in the computer-generated environment on-screen); or a simulation of presence in a computer-generated environment that treats the screen as a window frame through which one looks into a three-dimensional, virtual environment. A greater sense of "being inside" the environment could be obtained by using goggles instead of a video display and by including sounds and representations of the user's own hands on-screen via a data-glove.

The idea that "cyberspace" is a collective hallucination captures perfectly the socially created sense of space that exists via on-line media such as the World Wide Web. As a social construction, it is a unique collective phantasm that exists only in the minds of people, beyond sensory perception. It is an imagined totality which depends on the same cognitive processes invoked in us when we conceive of "the world" or "a continent" as a unit and as a whole. These concepts were also initially difficult to perceive, at least until the advent of photographs taken from outer space. Said another way, ideas such as a continent, a geographical region, or a nation are conjured in their absence on the basis of present indicators (Shields forthcoming). These concepts are thus "concrete abstractions" (cf. Lefebvre 1991; Shields 1999: 159–160). They are both a material product of human imagination and labor and a medium of social actions, because they structure and define the limits for subsequent activities. But they depend on an indexical leap from a fragment, which is encountered, to an abstract, absent totality, which is conjured.

Paul Virillio (1995) argues that conjuring cyberspace amounts to "a disturbance in the perception of what reality is," equating it to the invention of perspective rather than the discovery of the New World. Cyberspace requires a new form of "tactile perspective," which contributes to a loss of orientation. This has also been remarked upon by

Jameson (1984) and Lefebvre (1991), who both observed the postmodernizing effects that the development of global circuits of information and capital were having in everyday urban life:

> 14. A duplication of sensible reality, into reality and virtuality, is in the making. A stereo-reality of sorts threatens. A total loss of the bearings of the individual looms large. To exist, is to exist in situ, here and now. . . . This is precisely what is being threatened by cyberspace and instantaneous, globalized information flows. . . . .
> 16. . . . . To see at a distance, to hear at a distance: that was the essence of the audio-visual perspective of old. But to reach at a distance, to feel at a distance, that amounts to shifting the perspective towards a domain it did not yet encompass: that of contact, of contact-at-a-distance: tele-contact. (Virillio 1995)

For Virillio, the effect of a loss of orientation is felt in our relationship with others and the world at a distance. Nevertheless, perhaps the most enticing of current observations treats cyberspace as "something significant as the birth of cities," in Gibson's words. In this view, cyberspace is a substitute for urban space and experience (Boyer cited in Druckrey n.d.; see Boyer 1996), and perhaps even their replacement—a new way to "collectively manage ourselves on this planet" (Negroponte 1998). Perhaps future generations will see our visions of the twentieth-century city as constraining in their own way as the walled, medieval city might seem to us.

On the other hand, is cyberspace *really* like a city? Because of its scale, diversity, and the solitary involvement of users at their own individual computers, cyberspace feels politically neutral. Although it is possible to find virtual communities based on specialized interests (MGB automobile restorers, for example, or collectors of Devon lace-making bobbins), cyberspace appears for the most part to be a space not of assembly but of *assemblage*, whereby individuals are interrelated (in global, mega-audiences) without ever forming a mass.

Cities are "urban" because of their fundamental quality of both being sites of encounter (of coming together, of meeting) and hence of social centrality, as well as unbounded sites from which one departs (places one leaves or from which goods are transported). It is this quality of many simultaneous comings-together and goings-away that characterizes the phenomenology of the urban (Lefebvre 1972). The qualities we so value in cities are often related to being able to partake, even vicariously, in the collective frenzy of encounters, of arrivals and departures which we call—without analyzing it much—"bustle" or "the action." Great cities—London, Bangkok, Montreal—offer bystanders a sense of this through their provision of public spaces and street environments which the security- and privacy-obsessed interactions of cyberspace do not. Besides the loss of "seeing and being seen," there is the tactile history of the meeting, of exchange and of assembly. Are we really done with all that?

Of course, if cyberspace *is* the new equivalent of a city, it has its urban elite, as well as its homeless and poor. Cyberspace remains accessible only to the most wealthy and connected, most of whom live in the developed countries of the world. But maybe we need to understand cyberspace without prejudging it to be a city—or a world, or an auction hall, information highway, or stock exchange. A cultural economy of this "hallucination" may be needed to establish both the cultural processes by which understandings of on-line digital interaction and domains of data come to be spatialized as "cyberspace," and as a new form of the urban. Integrated with this cultural analysis, a political economy is needed—hence a "cultural economy" of the mechanisms by which power is exercised via actions on data and other elements in this space. We need a sense of both the construction of control and of normality in cyberspace, the operation of power and of its ungovernability: cyberspace's "other spaces." Both the chapter on "Governance" and that on "Political Economy" take up these themes.

Chapter 7

Governance

Timothy W. Luke

No matter who you are and where you sit in the digital domains of cyberspace, the issue of governance is unavoidable.

The impact of the Web on governance is only beginning to be understood by the citizens and rulers of modern nation-states. The proliferation of computer-mediated communications in today's global networks is reshaping our vision of individual political agency and collective government structure—visions inherited from the territorial nation-state since before the Industrial Revolution.

Inasmuch as culture can be viewed as the acts and artifacts shared communicatively by particular human groups, the Web provides many new groups with alternative modes of action and types of artifacts to organize social interactions, institutionalize political movements, and advance economic demands. The Web's sites are resources whose assignment, sale, and use generate a new challenge to governance: how to create, border, police, and use virtual spaces. The nationality of those spaces—and hence the legal jurisdictions, strategic alliances, cultural norms, and communal rituals which will prevail in them—is contested insofar as their operational effects can be simultaneously experienced everywhere and nowhere. If the governmentality problematic is, as Foucault claims, the challenge of conveniently arranging things and people to organize the conduct of conduct, then the Web poses tremendous new challenges to governance. This chapter explores the challenges posed specifically by the Web's deterritorializing capabilities. Optimists believe the Web will radically improve all aspects of human life; pessimists argue it will finally ruin most of what humans value; and neutralists see it changing nothing substantially even if it transforms things operationally. The goal of this chapter is to illustrate this spectrum of thinking about the Web and governance.

Digital Domains

In his exhaustive search through the new networking systems behind "network society," Manuel Castells marches through three volumes of *The Information Age: Economy, Society and Culture*, pulling together everything and everyone he believes is at work in today's global networks. He attempts to show how "a new world is taking shape in this end of millennium" out of the synergistic reactions,

> in the historical coincidence, around the late 1960s and mid-1970s, of three *independent* processes: the information technology revolution; the economic crisis of both capitalism and statism, and their subsequent restructuring; and the blooming of cultural social movements, such as libertarianism, human rights, feminism, and environmentalism. The interaction between these processes, and the reactions they triggered, brought into being a new dominant social structure, the network society; a new economy, the informational/global economy; and a new culture, the culture of real virtuality. (Castells 1998:336)

At the same time, this new world is greatly affected by older existing worlds in terms of its shape and substance, especially the dictates of capitalist exchange, nationalistic governance, and urbanized community. While these enduring forces remain in play, a new world order is now forming around the structures of "the network society." Not everything in this society accords with the design of informatic networks, but all societies are increasingly penetrated by the operational dynamics of such networks. Castells tends to overemphasize the extraordinary in these cultures of "real virtuality," but there are subtle shifts in the quirks of ordinary everyday life caused by the networking of existence. In fact, the proliferation of informatic networks becomes the background condition by which we explain how "real virtualities" are able to occupy the popular imagination of a cybernetic society:

On the one hand, dominant functions and values in society are organized in simultaneity without contiguity; that is, in flows of information that escape from the experience embodied in any locale. On the
other hand, dominant values and interests are constructed without reference to either past or future, in the timeless landscape of computer
networks and electronic media, where all expressions are either instan-
taneous, or without predictable sequencing. All expressions from all
times and from all spaces are mixed in the same hypertext, constantly
rearranged, and communicated at anytime, anywhere, depending on
the interests of senders and the moods of receivers. (Castells 1998:350)

This dizzy celebration of social relations in the grip of telematic
technoscience expresses the mood evoked by some in a network society. But, how exactly are the dominant functions and values of governance organized in terms of simultaneity on the timeless landscapes
of cybernetic connectivity? Castells suggests that everything can be
found blowing in the winds of hypertext. But there is much more to
the digital domain than this.

As individuals and groups now choose—or are coerced—to communicate, keep accounts, publish, buy products, work, access documents, or bank in the digital domain, this domain turns into the central setting for the conduct of individual human life (Luke 1998). It
defines and satisfies the range of needs that constitute forms of life as
well as the range of conduct most appropriate for satisfying these
needs (Jones 1993). On one level, cyberspace is clusters of code experienced on the network, but on another level it can be a portal into
new types of community, work, identity, sex, utility, knowledge, or
power. Wilson Dizard characterizes the networks of networks as "the
Meganet," or

a powerful but enigmatic engine of change, the biggest and most complex machine in human history. Its effects are paradoxically universal
and parochial, uniting and dividing, constructive and destructive. It
will create a new communications culture, overlaid on old ethnic, economic, religious, and national patterns and attitudes. An electronic environment is evolving in which old guideposts are submerged in a
stream of bits and bytes exchanging a bewildering variety of messages
among billions of individuals. (1997:14)

Unlike many celebrations of cyberspace, this view highlights the machinic infrastructure of boxes and wires, cables and satellites, servers

and relays that underpin the real built networks, which in turn generate new, hyperreal electronic environments (Deibert 1997). Both cry out for governance.

From Civil to Cyberian Society

As Castells indicates, the scope, pace, and direction of fundamental change in contemporary economies and societies today is often attributed to the ever-shifting technics of networked computing. At the same time, the remediation of cultural identity and political power through the interactions of humans and computers on networks is still conventionally reimagined in spatial terms. Rushkoff, for example, typifies an essentially millenarian reading of computer-mediated communication as a new ontological project for humanity:

> Welcome to Cyberia. Time seems to be speeding up. New ideas and technologies have accelerated our culture into an almost unrecognizable reality, and those on the frontier tell us that this is only the beginning. . . . Now that PCs are linked through networks that cover the globe and beyond, many people spend real time out there in "cyberspace"—the territory of digital information. This apparently boundless universe of data breaks all of the rules of physical reality. People can interact regardless of time and location. They can fax "paper" over phone lines, conduct twenty-party video-telephone conversations with participants in different countries, and even "touch" one another from thousands of miles away through new technologies such as virtual reality. All of this and more can happen in cyberspace. (Rushkoff 1994:2)

Cyberspace in such rhetoric is much more than mere technical effects. It mutates into a new plane of cultural reality with its own rules of postmodern embodiment, extraterritorial engagement, and hyperreal enlightenment. Everything allegedly changes in cyberian society, including the old rules of cultural, economic, and political interaction. So new types of human beings with their own special forms of society are also seen as emerging with the interface. Rushkoff sees these savvy cybernetic individuals as Cyberia's inhabitants, "the cyberians, who are characterized primarily by faith in their ability to consciously rechoose their own reality—to design their experience of life" (Rushkoff 1994:4).

Governance of the Internet, however, is an emergent process that has not stepped very far beyond the juridical assumptions of off-line sovereignty over living bodies occupying physical territories. Who rules whom, what is ruled how, and where rules begin and end are all open questions at this time in cyberspace. Much of the Net was made to work without a powerful ruler and will be beyond continual rulings once the basic TCP/IP rules of packet switching are accepted. This openness, distributedness, decentralization, and interactivity creates environments bounded by connectivity, interactivity, freedom, and autonomy. The fundamental Netiquettes of on-line cultures and network economics impose some boundary conditions of operation, though these are very weak means of governing our collective activities. Nonetheless, the proponents of Internet life, like Rushkoff, believe they are more than enough.

In cyberian society, according to those with utopian views, the technics of computer-mediated communication are simultaneously technological and political mechanisms suitable for redirecting individual and collective behavior in preparation for "man's leap out of history altogether and into the timeless dimension of Cyberia" (Rushkoff 1994:4). The cybertopes of cyberian living are also sites where the certainties of ordinary reality, as millions have come to know it, will no longer hold true, because they are fading into the open, multitasked flexible operations of the digital domain (Seabrook 1997).

In his typically unaffected fashion Bill Gates outlines his version of these wide-ranging changes in the built environments of contemporary economies and societies by recounting his, and supposedly everyone else's, experience of "growing up" with computers:

> In the minds of a lot of people at school we became linked with the computer, and it with us. . . . It seems there was a whole generation of us, all over the world, who dragged that favorite toy with us into adulthood. In doing so, we caused a kind of revolution—peaceful, mainly—and now the computer has taken up residence in our offices and homes. . . . Inexpensive computer chips now show up in engines, watches, antilock brakes, facsimile machines, elevators, gasoline pumps, cameras, thermostats, treadmills, vending machines, burglar alarms, and even talking greeting cards. . . . Now that computing is astoundingly inexpensive and computers inhabit every part of our lives, we stand on the brink of another revolution. This one will involve unprecedently inexpensive

communication; all the computers will join together to communicate with us and for us. . . . There will be a day, not far distant, when you will be able to conduct business, study, explore the world and its cultures, call up any great entertainment, make friends, attend neighborhood markets, and show pictures to distant relatives—without leaving your desk or armchair. You won't leave your network connection behind at the office or in the classroom. It will be more than an object you carry or an appliance you purchase. (Gates 1995:2–5)

For Gates, and, of course, Microsoft, computers remake built environments. Economies and societies change as computers connect to us, computers mature with us, computers reside with us at home, computers work with us in the office, computers colonize many other technical artifacts for us, computers integrate us into networks, and computers create new multimediated ways of life. Without saying so, Gates essentially suggests that computers and networks have acquired the qualities of an environment: networks, like the ecologies of nature, are always beneath, behind, and beyond the political order of our civic life. This revolution, as it is made from desktops and laptops, coevolves with, and within, a new built environment, fabricated out of bits, mediated over networks, and located on-line.

Bill Gates looks down his cybernetic "road ahead" and sees the coming of "friction-free" marketplaces where Says' Law is finally fulfilled: what is supplied will be in demand, while what is in demand can be supplied. In fact, he believes that "we may be about to witness the realization of Adam Smith's perfect market, at last" (Gates 1995:4). When Gates envisions this perfected "friction-free capitalism" of Adam Smith on the Net, he sees the wired world's coming digital exchanges in exultant terms:

The global information market will be huge and will combine all the various ways human goods, services and ideas are exchanged. On a practical level, this will give you broader choices about most things, including how you earn and invest, what you buy and how much you pay for it, who your friends are and how you spend your time with them, and where and how securely you and your family live. Your workplace and your idea of what it means to be "educated" will be transformed, perhaps almost beyond recognition. Your identity, of who you are and where you belong, may open up considerably. In short, just about everything will be done differently. (1995:6–7)

Under this cosmopolitan horizon, Gates asks everyone to head out on the information superhighways to find and fulfill their needs. At this triumphalist juncture in the evolving capitalist world system, the workings of collective authority seem to be shifting from a strongly centered territorial logic of nation-states set-in-place into a weakly decentered telematic logic of corporate organization managed in global markets just-in-time (Luke 1989).

At the same time, Gates's "wired world" is much more than just its boxes and wires: it is an entirely new product space. It is an entirely new market space. The Internet product space, combined with the World Wide Web market space, establishes one of the most powerful platforms ever contrived for doing business. The Wired World is to the friction-free economy what the interstate highway system, air cargo system, and telephone/fax system were to the old economy (Lewis 1997:115).

Even though its enthusiasts continue to effuse over "a near-infinite supply of products, services, and ideas" that this friction-free economy apparently produces "at near-zero cost" (Lewis 1997:115), the modularized acceleration of goods and services is not generating Gates's friction-free economy as much as it is transmuting civil into cyberian society.

Informatics as a "Subpolis"

While political philosophers often see elements of the common good running through public projects underpinning the territorial polis, different agendas tied to private profit and power sustain what might be called the "informatic subpolis." The subpolis lies uncomfortably somewhere between politics and nonpolitics. As Beck suspects, informatic systems, like cybernetic networks, telecommunications grids, or computer applications become

> a third entity, acquiring the precarious hybrid status of a *sub-politics*, in which the scope of social changes precipitated varies inversely with their legitimization. . . . The direction of development and results of technological transformation become fit for discourse and subject to legitimization. Thus business and techno-scientific action acquire a *new political and moral dimension* that had previously seemed alien to techno-

economic activity. . . . [N]ow the potential for structuring society mi-
grates from the political system into the sub-political system of scientific, technological, and economic modernization. *The political becomes
non-political and the non-political political.* . . . A revolution under the
cloak of normality occurs, which escapes from possibilities of intervention, but must all the same be justified and enforced against a public becoming critical. . . . The political institutions become the administrators
of a development they neither have planned for nor are able to structure, but must nevertheless somehow justify. (Beck 1992:186–187)

Gates, and thousands of other much more anonymous computer
people like him, are conducting a revolution in governance from their
desktops by designing new subpolitical spaces for cyberian society.
Of course, the cybertopes of the Web, the Wintel operating system, or
the ASCII code, are often neither foreseen nor wanted before their advent; but decisions made by technicians and tradesmen to structure
society around such "subpolitical systems of scientific, technological,
and economic modernization" (Beck 1992:186) are changing the
world without much, if any, political planning, state structure, or
civic legitimization. (See "Political Economy," this volume.)

As this informatic subpolis grows, the role and stature of the traditional polis may well decline. Even though everyone currently remains within some type of face-to-face political system, many are losing their civic ability to exercise the practice of rule making, rule applying, and rule adjudication to the subpolitical domains of technics.
Democracy off-line may become an engine of collective inaction or,
worse, the audience for endless spectacles of quasi-theatrical scandal.
In turn, the decisive revolutions that can be made in cyberian society,
as Beck argues, occur *"under the cloak of normality"* (1992:186) thanks
to agents like Microsoft and Bill Gates. Indeed, Gates's narratives of
informatic transformation simply illustrate how on-line governmentality operates through subpolitical conduits (Madden 1998:64–69).
"In contemporary discussions," as Beck suggests, "the 'alternative society' is no longer expected to come from parliamentary debates on
new laws, but rather from the application of microelectronics, genetic
technology, and information media" (1992:223).

Even Bill Gates recognizes that the rudimentary terrain of cyberian
society no longer has much objective necessity (after all, he calls the
computer "that favorite toy" [Gates 1995:3] of a conflicted generation
dragged into adulthood on-line). Second, it brims with choice, as all

its operative rules require a new pluralism tied to open-source initial decisions and ongoing technical revisions of past decisions. That is, all users of informatic technology collaborate with Microsoft, IBM, Cisco, and others to build, maintain, and then rebuild the multilayered digital domains of the computer-mediated subpolis. Once there, network connectivity oddly becomes "your passport into 'a new, mediated way of life'" (Gates 1995:5). Like cities in civilization, networks increasingly form the larger piece of where we live, and we cannot leave them behind. More than an object, yet not quite a subject, computer connectivity simultaneously provides one a pass, a port, and a presence for entering into this new way of life.

Governmentality in Digital Domains

In many ways, cyberspace is a place of pure governance. Its orderly ones and zeros are devoted to systemic steering, generalized governmentality, and operational order. (See "Multimedia," this volume.) Because the hardware and software sets that generate the Net's functionalities are organized around particular rules, these clusters of tools and codes also possess peculiar ruling properties. Their design, order, and impact all presort the number and range of possible behaviors in the on-line environment. Through them, anonymous cohorts of code writers and machine builders exert their rule at a distance over on-line behavior; consequently, these cyberian interests determine in some sense what can, and cannot, be done on-line.

Telematic technologies are now emerging as the decisive new political technology that has, in turn, invested the whole space of human existence, technical performance, and market exchange with its own command, control, communication, and intelligence functions. Cyberspace now constitutes another kind of built environment on-line within familiar built environments off-line set amidst the natural environment. Getting access from this space, gaining leverage for it, and giving significance to it can all be relations of radical empowerment, although the networks are closed proprietary structures requiring a considerable investment in private property and the spending of money. The hands that mark up the code, run the cable, and fabricate the computer now make the connections between things and people—and this conduct takes place through the cash nexus. Network connectivity requires, and then remediates, govern-mentality effects in its tools, technics, and techniques of operation.

As Foucault portrays the practical arts of government, ruling forces introduce a rational economy about the management of things into the political practices of state institutions (Foucault 1991:93). Sig-nificantly, Foucault sees expert authorities in the state bureaucracies and corporate firms mobilizing systems of surveillance and control to bring about "the emergence of population as a datum, as a field of in-tervention and as an objective of governmental techniques, and the process which isolates the economy as a specific sector of reality" (Foucault 1991:102). Once defined in these lattices of analysis, "the population is the object that government must take into account in all its observations and *savior*, in order to be able to govern effectively in a rational and conscious manner" (Foucault 1991:100).

Individuals and groups become fully enmeshed within the tactics and strategies of complex forms of normalizing power whose institu-tions, procedures, analyses, and techniques loosely organize mass populations and their material environments in several different highly politicized symbolic and material economies. The government provides an inexact set of bearings, but Foucault asserts:

> it is the tactics of government which make possible the continual defin-ition and redefinition of what is within the competence of the state and what is not, the public versus the private, and so on; thus the state can only be understood in its survival and its limits on the basis of the gen-eral tactics of governmentality. (Foucault 1991:103)

Because governmentalizing techniques are always the central focus of political struggle and contestation, the interactions of populations with their natural surroundings in highly politicized consumer economies compel regimes to redefine what is within their adminis-trative competence throughout the modernizing process.

To survive in the capitalist world of the 1990s, it is not enough for territorial states merely to maintain legal jurisdiction off-line over their allegedly sovereign territories. The Net is a governmentality en-gine whose subpolitical assemblies of informatic artifacts create new collective subjectivities and collections of subjects. The workings of on-line disciplinary practices in turn can be reevaluated as "the ele-ment in which are articulated, the effects of a certain type of power and the reference of a certain type of knowledge, the machinery by which the power relations give rise to a possible corpus of knowledge, and knowledge extends and reinforces the effects of this power" (Foucault 1979:29). In on-line governmentality, the disciplinary articulations of software packages and hardware functionalities center upon establishing and enforcing "the right disposition of things" between humans conducting their conduct in their cybernetic environments. (See "Ideology," this volume.)

Once on-line agency emerges as a social project for network administration, the statistical attitudes of corporate product demography diffuse into the numerical surveillance of the Net's many layers of networked connectivity. Many agencies of governmentality, then, can begin to preoccupy themselves with "the conduct of conduct" in networks. Until now, the off-line involvement of family, community, and nation has guided our conduct; at this juncture, Internet economies and societies seek to be accepted as another ethical ground for normalizing an individual's behavior. Cybernetic domains are spaces under a special kind of self-policing supervision, self-managing expertise, or self-regulating technics. By reading the Net's communal (dis)order into the heart of digital being, one finds the ultimate meaning of its self-policing fulfilled. The immense promise of material prosperity looming ahead on a global scale would not be possible without this new governmentality to guide "the controlled insertion of bodies into the machinery of production and the adjustment of the phenomena of population to economic processes" (Foucault 1980:141). Yet, a digital politics rooted in telematic hardware, software, content, and connectivity providers can respecify the range of governmentality, as packets of bits remediate "the methods of power capable of optimizing forces, aptitudes, and life in general without at the same time making them more difficult to govern" (Foucault 1980:141).

Telecracy: Rule Over/Through Bits

Telecracy is rule at a distance through faraway rulings by faraway rulers. Even though the Net is plainly a collective enterprise, built by thousands to be used by millions, there is the impulse to center its powers upon someone. Those who invent and control the technologies of the Net build the subpolis, and telecratic rule is exerted through, within, and because of the technics comprising the subpolis.

No one better represents the telecrat at this juncture than Bill Gates, and no enterprise captures the qualities of telecracy more fully than Microsoft. This conflict of the polis and subpolis, in turn, is at the heart of the ongoing U.S. Department of Justice proceedings against Microsoft for allegedly committing serious antitrust violations in its software design and sales strategies (Hirsh 1998:42–43). Telecrats whose powers can be separated and balanced are more palatable than those whose authority is undisputed and power concentrated, and Bill Gates's business has been very adept at consolidating functions and bundling capabilities that constrain one to behave in certain Microsoft-approved ways from the boot-up screen to the shut-down command.

Because Bill Gates's "road ahead" is one that Microsoft wants to own and control, the issue of ruling over and through bits assumes considerable importance. The 1999 Department of Justice antitrust suit against Gates and his corporation recognized this fact in its wide-ranging finding about many monopolistic practices in the ways that the Redmond, Washington, based firm has packaged and sold its Windows software package. Microsoft has enjoyed a virtual fifteen-year monopoly over billions of income every year. Despite the best efforts of Apple, AT&T/Lucent, DEC, Oracle, and SUN, Microsoft's software applications still dominate the world's PCs, occupying over 90 percent of all desktops (Wilke and Bank 1998:B1).

In Microsoft's defense, Gates presented himself and his firm not as monopoly makers but rather as monopoly breakers, because, when he began working on Microsoft Basic during the 1970s in his Harvard dorm room, IBM was the evil empire that controlled most of the world's computing. Thanks to Microsoft, IBM's stranglehold was broken, and in turn, "the statistics show that the cost of computing has decreased ten million fold since 1971. That's the equivalent of getting Boeing 747 for the price of a pizza" (Wilke and Bank 1998:B1).

Whether Microsoft is an evil empire or not, and whether or not Microsoft's dominance over software has led computing power prices to fall to a level where jumbo jet capabilities now arrive at the price of a Domino's home delivery, these are vital questions. Their asking illustrates how worried people are becoming about governance issues that arise from subpolitical choices, like "the lock-in" for informatic goods: "What we *do not see* and *do not* want is changing the world"

(Beck 1992:187). The subpolis develops with each new corporate move made by cybernetic telecrats, like Gates, and their rule from afar can change the most mundane details of how everyday life is conducted.

By fabricating digital domains, and then continuously struggling to master their informatic terrain, cyberian interests fulfill Jean-Francois Lyotard's prophecies about "the postmodern condition." That is, "knowledge in the form of an informational commodity indispensable to productive power is already, and will continue to be, a major—perhaps *the* major—stake in the worldwide competition for power." In fact, the intranational and transnational struggle over cyberspace illustrates how fully the residents of civil society in nation-states must fight interests in the nascent terrain of cyberian society for "control of information, just as they battled in the past for control over territory, and afterwards for control of access to and exploitation of raw materials and cheap labor" (1984:5). On-line governance now works through protocols for the processing and reprocessing of data, information, and knowledge in its telematic forms. On-line and off-line, information "is and will be produced in order to be sold, it is and will be consumed in order to be valorized in a new production: in both cases, the goal is exchange" (Lyotard 1984:4). In another register, Nicholas Negroponte continuously touts the potentialities of these changes as the state of "being digital" (1995:11–20). Indeed, he celebrates digitalization as the latest grand transition of modernization: the shift from a society organized around making and moving matter, or "atoms," who often congregate in grounded democracies to one focused upon inventing and integrating information, or "bits," which flow through the links of cyberian society. Yet, being digital, as Lyotard observes, also implies that everything in society and the marketplace

> is made conditional on performativity. The redefinition of the norms of life consists in enhancing the system's competence for power. That this is the case is particularly evident in the introduction of telematic technology: the technocrats see in telematics a promise of liberalization and enrichment in the interactions between interlocutors; but what makes this process attractive for them is that it will result in new tensions in the system, and these will lead to an improvement in its performativity. (Lyotard 1984:64)

The social pragmatics of performativity, or means-ends cost efficiency, slowly supplant more deeply embedded narratives of meaning, or essential human rights, elegant moral duties, enduring social contracts. As loosely defined just-in-time protocols for building fluid temporary arrangements begin to prevail in governance, more impermanent understandings of personal rights and social obligations come into vogue in our public life because of their "greater flexibility, lower cost, and the creative turmoil of its accompanying motivations—all of these factors contribute to increased operativity" (Lyotard 1984:66).

Cybertopes: Cites as Sites

Castells indicates how "information technology became the indispensable tool for the effective implementation of socio-economic restructuring," but he is much less specific about "the development of networking as a dynamic, self-expanding form of organization of human activity" (1998:336–337). Because networks are simultaneously the most basic means of economic production as well as the fullest expression of cultural sophistication, the operational base of cybernetic technology provides that measure of "simultaneity without contiguity" needed to police real-life places from the virtuality of cyberspace. Being granted access to them is a measure of systemic significance, while closing access off to others marks the increasing irrelevance of those denied. Castells sees informational capitalist development, network economies and societies as new zones of exclusivity where "capital, labor, information, and markets linked up, through technology, valuable functions, people, and localities around the world, while switching off from their networks those populations and territories deprived of value and interest for the dynamics of global capitalism" (1998:337). Thus the subpolitical realm of telematics totally remakes the political textures of world governance.

On one level, the Internet is neither governed nor even governable. Cyberspace exists within, but also separate and apart from, ordinary national territories. Consequently, the Internet has been, and mostly still is, a very good example of a working "anarchy" whose largely decentralized bottom-up governance has followed from the openness of its TCP/IP protocols. Within now commonly accepted technical standards, the packet switching protocols of the Net allow anyone everywhere to communicate easily, economically, and expeditiously with everyone anywhere as long as they have connectivity and acknowledge these standards. Of course, the material e-structures of telecommunication grids, data network systems, and personal computing solutions off-line are all subject to regulation by various governments and domination by big corporations. However, the virtual structures of cyberspace itself on-line are proving much more difficult to control.

On this second level, then, the Internet is becoming a highly contested site as those who favor individual freedom experiment with new modes of distributed popular governance in cyberspace, while those who see individual choices being foreclosed want to test new systems of focused popular resistance against informatics. The technics of the Net can be shaped to serve many purposes, ranging from more open popular self-governance to more closed expert social control. There are tendencies toward both directions already developing, but their original inspirations and ultimate influences are often quite surprising (Ohmae 1990).

Because telecracy in cyberian society is rule at a distance, gaining control over the digital environments in which people communicate with others, conduct their business, buy many products, and acquire new knowledge constitutes a new mode of technologically mediated, network-carried, and software-enforced governance. All these relations are embedded in complex networks; therefore, the common presumption is that purely technical imperatives cause them to take this form over that, to operate here rather than there, on any number of considerations. Yet most of these technical decisions are made on aesthetic, commercial, financial, social, or political grounds instead of purely engineering criteria. Thus, the aesthetic prejudices, commercial aspirations, financial targets, political beliefs, or social fears of the hardware designers, software vendors, and network providers shape the domain of permissible behaviors. No matter who you are or where you sit in the digital domains of cyberspace, the issue of governance is unavoidable; informatic telecrats dictate how your cybernetic conduct will be conducted and what you can do from where you are by shaping the on-line environments you access.

Chapter 8

Ideology

John M. Sloop

> Profitable products and popular Web pages must reinforce the "common sense" that consumers already recognize and have taken on as their own.

In an essay that seeks to define "ideology" for students of literary studies, James Kavanagh makes a number of useful observations. First, he notes that ideology cannot be defined as the opposite of "common sense" or as the opposite of "realism" because all understandings, all knowledge, all "sense" *is ideological*. Indeed our most basic common sense is grounded on our culture's most fundamental knowledges. As Kavanagh writes, ideology is "a social process that works on and through every social subject. . . . like any other social process, everyone is 'in,' whether or not they 'know' or understand it" (1990:311). In other words, ideology, like its cousin term "discourse," refers to the process by which knowledge of self and of the world is created, maintained, and assumed. Kavanagh goes on to suggest that ideological analysis, the task of literary and cultural critics, investigates the ways that such lived relations as class, race, and sex are constituted and transformed, as well as affiliated with various politics. Hence, ideological analysis, which readers of *Unspun* are engaged in, concerns both coming to understand the ways knowledge about self, others, and the world is constituted, *and* working to change various elements of such knowledge.

Such a definition of both ideology and ideological analysis seems particularly fitting when we turn our attention to the World Wide

Web. Given that the Internet—and now the Web, which, along with email, is the most frequently used component of the Internet—has come to be understood in common vernacular as *the* information superhighway, a location where one can learn anything one wants to (and a lot more), the Web seems to beg for analysis. If "ideology" is made up of what counts as knowledge, a site like the Web, which is increasingly a location for nearly all information, is being positioned as the bank of cultural knowledge and hence of ideology. This connection between ideology (or knowledge) and the Web has a number of interesting strands, three of which I will pursue in this chapter. While these three connections overlap in part, distinctions are useful for thinking through the role of criticism.

First, "the Web" itself is an object of cultural discourse and is given meaning through the lens of ideology. That is, the way "the Web" (and, more generally, the Internet) is talked about in private discussions, in advertising, in political speeches, in literature, in films, and in other sites of cultural conversation determines in large part what the Web means to each of us and how each of us will approach it. Second, like all discourse, one can investigate the ways that language, visuals, and assumptions existing on the Web itself (its content) are themselves ideological and are complicit or resistant to dominant ideology (and open for ideological critique) in the same way that all discourses are. Third, as critics, we need to consider the ways in which the dominant media through which we communicate affect or influence what is communicated; in this case, the Web as a dominant means of communication affects ideology in the sense that it transforms the way we think, what we think about, and how we constitute our own identities.

Since its inception, the Internet has been discussed and understood through multiple metaphors: the "information superhighway," "the matrix," "the Web," and so on. From advertising, we learn that the Web will allow us to go anywhere and be anything, free from the constraints of age, gender, infirmity, sexuality, time, and space. Indeed, the Web is said to allow travel to any place, at any time, under any identity. One way in which ideological analysis about the World Wide Web might proceed, then, is to think through some of the ways that discussions or configurations of the Web are themselves ideological. Relying on what might be referred to as a Forrest Gump theory of ideology and meaning (that is, "X is as X does"), we can think of the meaning of the Web as equal to what the term means in conversation and in popular cultural discussions. As David and Ann Gunkel put it, "What cyberspace becomes will, to a great extent, depend on what we call it" (1997:133). If cyberspace becomes whatever it is called, it seems imperative, then, that we become *aware and involved* in what we call the Web and what that ultimately means.

For instance, if the Web is talked about as a location in which gender, race, sexuality, and class disappear as markers of identity, as a utopia where each of us can be whatever we want to be, we ultimately circumvent our ability to think about the ways in which race, class, gender, and sexuality continue to operate ideologically. A class I recently taught that focused on identity and the Internet starkly brought this point to light. In a rather vibrant discussion one afternoon, an African American male student, excited by the "be whatever you want to be" discourse, observed that one of the strengths of the Web was that he could be anything he wanted while on-line; as an illustration, he noted, "In chatrooms and in letters, I can be an Asian female if I like." It was a particularly interesting moment in class as the other students pursued the discussion in the direction of imagining themselves talking "on-line" to an Asian female while they were really talking to their fellow student. When asked about the differences that might take place in the conversation given the two different understandings of their conversational partner, the students drew upon a number of stock stereotypes of Asian femininity in imagining the conversation. Moreover, the stereotypes worked in a particularly hypersexualized way for the heterosexual men in the class. Ultimately, the class discovered that just because one could "claim" (and attempt to perform) Asian femaleness regardless of one's own understanding of one's race, gender, and identity, doing so did very little to disrupt the cultural meanings of "femininity," "Asianness," or the intersections between the two. Instead, the meanings clustered around these categories were reified by the performance. Significantly, we learned that the utopian discourse of freedom would work to unhinge our ability to criticize sexism, racism, classism, and the like unless we were careful about thinking through both "freedom" and complicity.

Thinking about the Web in a utopian manner creates other ideological problems. For example, if we picture the Web as a location for an emerging democratic *polis* that encourages a greater inclusion of marginal interests into a larger conversation, we discourage focusing on

"The Web has allowed a public space for a wide array of competing and marginal interests." About.com site. http://www.about.com

the ways in which some voices continue to be privileged over others, and the ways in which capital and the metaphorical and literal financing of popular Web pages continue to have a shaping influence on the Web's content. Further, if one understands the Web as a location in which the world becomes one community (a global village), one forgets the ways in which this one community draws primarily upon English and the interests of Western culture in the construction of this smaller world. As a final utopian example, when one uses the metaphor of the superhighway, one envisions the Web as linear, with autonomous individuals following their individual interests, picking up objective knowledge on their journey. Such a metaphor ignores, of course, the complexity of identity and the perspectival character of knowledge.

With almost equal rhetorical force, there are numerous dystopic articulations of the Web which, like their utopic counterparts, ultimately shape the way we interact with the Web. Examples of dystopic visions are widespread in discourses about the Web. The Web is variously pointed to as a site through which millennial groups recruit and brainwash followers, a metaphoric street corner where pedophiles recruit and abuse children, a hyperporn arcade in which images of sexual debauchery work to pervert America's youth, and, grounded in news events, a meeting place where trench coat mafioso reinforce each others' hatreds, learn to build bombs, and slaughter classmates. In these representations of the Web, an ideology about what the Web "means" (its corrupting nature) reinforces and rearticulates assumed cultural values and assumed cultural knowledge. That is, like the utopic visions, the dystopic ones perpetuate existing logics, values, and knowledge.

My point is that the ways in which we talk about the Web *creates* the Web as an object of knowledge and morals, situating it within our dominant ideology. As Ann and David Gunkel point out, despite the fact that the Web is discussed as part of a "new world," our discourse of newness must necessarily draw upon metaphors from the "old world" in building its case. Like all other objects of discourse, the Web and its meanings are constrained by the ways we talk about it, and the ways that we talk about the Web in part constrains who we are and what we can be.

Second, not only are the ways that we talk about the Web shaped by the dominant ideology, but the dominant ideology is in turn shaped by those ways of talking about it. Further, the content of the Web itself is already ideological, and favors particular and predictable interests. On the one hand, as I observed above, the Web has allowed a public space for a wide array of competing and marginal interests ranging from fringe political groups to fringe sexual practices to marginal music and food interests. Indeed, ideologically there is something to celebrate about the proliferation of transgressive ideologies, transgressive beliefs about what counts as knowledge, and transgressive moralities. Of course, given a critic's own political systems and political goals (mine, in this case), there are clearly going to be both specific behaviors and discourses on the Web that one will want to celebrate or condemn. But the very existence of increased availability and visibility of alternate voices and worldviews (within the limits of those who have access to the Web) should be seen as positive for those, like myself, who hold that the disruption of dominant ideologies is beneficial.

On the other hand, observers and critics of the Web would be remiss if they chose to celebrate the Web as if it operated largely as a free marketplace of ideas, a *polis* with competing logics engaged in a fair and equal battle. The problems with such a perspective are multiple. For one thing, to the degree that those who are writing and reading Web documents are part of a larger "dominant" culture, their writing and reading practices are shaped by the knowledge (and ideologies) assumed by the logic of the dominant culture. That is, each of us, as both consumers and producers of Web content, take to the Web the assumptions we had before the Web existed, before we encountered it. We are as likely to be dismissive of a "fringe" opinion on the Web as we would be if we heard it spoken aloud at a dinner conversation.

In addition, because the Web has become more market driven over the years, the content of the Web has become more mainstreamed, more ideologically in line with the assumptions of dominant culture. Because so many Web pages are either financed through advertising or links to other commercial sites, and because so many Web pages are attempting to increase their number of hits (the presence of counters on Web pages with no economic incentives attests to the desire of some Web page owners to attract large numbers of readers), the discourse (that is, the topics, the tone, the assumptions, the language, the images) on such pages must closely match with the "common sense" of their readers. While we can obviously point to cases of innovation and transition, and while the Web has perhaps more space for change than other media, I want to suggest that just as profitable products—television shows, clothing, automobiles, and so on—have to be useful to consumers, so do pages on the Web that hope to attract a large number of viewers. Profitable products and popular Web pages must reinforce the "common sense" that consumers already recognize and have taken on as their own. As rhetoricians have known since humans made their first utterances, audiences are attracted to messages that are about them, about their concerns and interests. So whether it is a page encouraging hits by a vast array of consumers or a page meant for a niche audience, both must ideologically reaffirm the beliefs of its audience and in so doing reaffirm specific kinds of knowledge and values.

Whether it is cnnsi.com providing mainstream news and sports or the No Depression Web page providing "commonsense" understandings of alternative country music, each page reifies particular types of knowledge, particular ways of understanding the world. While always allowing small changes in understanding (ideology is, after all, always an equilibrium in transition), this automatic maintenance of the dominant ideology is an example of what John Fiske and John Hartley refer to as "ideological clawback" (1978:87). In their example regarding television, they note that nature programs often stress the ways that animals are "like us" or "unlike us" in order to provide behavioral equivalencies that allow the viewer to organize the activities of the subject in ways that are common and acceptable to him or her. Regardless of whether the animal is "like" or "unlike" us, our way of organizing behavior and reality becomes the norm against which other behaviors parallel or differ. Similarly, if a site of discourse—whether it is a Web page or a musical recording—is to offer a critique of the dominant ideology, it must first be understandable within that ideology if a substantial audience is going to be able to "make sense" of it. As a result, any critique, any shift in meaning, reifies a large portion of the dominant discourse while offering small segments of change. Although there is always space for change and transition in the discourse of the Web, the space is persistently and automatically being closed, just as it is outside the Web, by the need to be intelligible.

As Thomas Swiss (2000) points out in a study of music-fan Web pages, even pages that are not ostensibly driven by economic benefits (that is, have no advertising, and are designed and maintained by fans) are often shaped *as if they were* driven by economic benefits and hence do similar ideological work. In interviewing fans who had "unofficial" Web pages designed to honor their favorite musicians, Swiss discovered that many fans designed their pages to appear as if they were "official" Web pages. This was done either because they wanted them to be picked up as official pages at some point by the band or its label or simply because they wanted the page to appear "official" (and hence, trustworthy), even if they meant to maintain control over the page. If we assume that something similar occurs with other "fan" pages, we again see that even when pages are not directly or currently driven by economic interests, the overall effect of trying to appear "normal" and "professional" produces Web pages that in the end reify dominant understandings, assumptions, and ideology.

Finally, a third way of thinking about the relationship between the World Wide Web and ideology is to think through the relationship between cultural consciousness and dominant media forms. In his classic and prophetic text, *Understanding Media: The Extensions of Man*, Marshall McLuhan noted the primacy of technological form over content by observing that "In terms of the ways in which the machine altered our relations to one another and to ourselves, it mattered not in the least whether it turned out cornflakes or Cadillacs" (1964:8). Claiming that "the medium is the message," McLuhan helps us focus more directly on the relationship between a culture's dominant mode of communication and its influence on "our relations to one another and to ourselves." McLuhan helps us understand how a culture's dominant means of communication (from orality to literacy to print to electronic to digital) act as an extension of the "self" across temporal and spatial boundaries. Framing media form as an extension of the human being, we can then ask how form influences self and society. Hence, while McLuhan and other scholars and historians of orality and literacy—like Walter Ong (1982) and Eric Havelock (1986)—have theorized the ways in which transitions from dominantly oral cultures to dominantly literate and print cultures or dominantly electronic cultures have altered how the self was thought of and how knowledge was conceived, a contemporary media theorist might be interested in how digital communication and the Web as an "extension of man" [*sic*] shapes our knowledge of self and others. In short, he or she would want to know how current dominant media shape our ideology.

This line of thinking asks questions that are both epistemological (what do we know? what can we know?) and ontological (what are "we"?). As a result, if we are to paraphrase McLuhan when thinking about the relationship between ideology and the Web, we might put it this way: "In terms of our relations to one another and to ourselves, it matters not in the least whether Web pages contain pornography or popular music." That is, if we are to take a media theory look at the Web, we are interested in the ways in which the Web, as it becomes a dominant means of communication, alters *what* we can know about ourselves and our world and *how* we can know.

Perhaps one of McLuhan's more celebrated concepts, the "global village," can help us understand the relationship between the Web and ideology. In explaining the global village, McLuhan first explained that in oral societies, people by necessity clustered around each other in tribal units and understood themselves, first and foremost, in terms of the group, unable to identify as a "self" completely separate from the group. With the advent of writing and later of print media, the thoughts and ideas of "individuals" were allowed not only to be externalized from the body and mind but also to be left to stand alone spatially and temporally (that is, as extensions of the human being). This in turn allowed the reproduction and eventual copyright of these ideas, thereby reifying the individual as a free-standing and separate self. Moreover, given that ideas could be reflected upon and analyzed regardless of their use, literacy and print encouraged a far greater degree of rational thought, linear knowledge, and striated thinking.[1] With the arrival of electronic mass communication such as television, we once again see transitions in epistemology and ontology. Not only do we witness a move back to more "emotional" thinking as a form of proof in public argument, but television allows us to "see" the condition of other human beings throughout the world, hence encouraging us to think of ourselves as part of one community (the global village) rather than a multiplicity of cultures clearly delineated by national borders.

In sum, such a theory argues that while literacy and print encouraged the growth of the individual and the rise of community boundaries, television encourages not only a greater group consciousness but also the renewal of an emotional and smooth epistemology over a rational and striated one. In McLuhan's language, what is communicated on television is in large part the product of television itself rather than separate "objective" content.

If we think about this link between media and ideology in terms of the Internet and the Web, we can make several observations about how the Internet as a form shapes cultural assumptions and understandings. In terms of individual versus group thought, we can speculate that as a dominant mode of communication, the Internet will encourage a cultural move toward what might be called a fragmented global village. That is, while the Internet certainly encourages us to think of ourselves as linked to a number of different "communities" or identities that exist on a global level, we are simultaneously transformed in our relations with those living geographically near us. For example, I am a member of a number of listservs dealing with such topics as masculinity, Throwing Muses, T. Rex, and communication studies; I also play an active role in other on-line communities such as backgammon. While I have rarely physically met any of the people involved in any of these communities (indeed, I might add, for the most part I would actively avoid physically meeting many of these on-line "friends"), my identity as an individual is to some degree constituted by my membership in these groups. One of the consequences of my having established myself within on-line communities that match my interests is that I have less need to constitute myself as a member of communities with those living right next door to me. While there are clearly reasons why I will in fact have relationships and interests with physical neighbors, these relationships are changed to some degree. My subjectivity is constituted through a number of global identities, communities existing in cyberspace, and identities that encourage psychic distance between myself and those living closest to me. (See "Identity," this volume, for more thoughts on this subject.)

As suggested above, it has been repeatedly argued that the transition from electronic culture to digital and Internet dominance will be accompanied by a move away from rational and linear forms of thinking—those with a prepared sequence of beginning, middle, and end. A more freely floating consciousness will emerge that encourages one to follow one's interests (that is, hyperlinking on the Web encourages one to regard thinking as opened-ended without assuming a particular *telos*) and to be an active agent in the creation of texts and their meanings. Examples of this are numerous: on amazon.com, a person can be one of hundreds of people who has chosen to write a review of a book; on any interest group on the Web, one can provide comments and criticism; with hypertextual novels, one can create one's own links. In this way, texts are forced not only to be a bit more fluid in meaning, but to be seen or read as fluid. As the chapter in this volume on "Hypertext" notes, we will increasingly understand texts as always being in transition, never stable in meaning or place but also never completely fluid.

In terms of knowledge about our "selves" and our "individuality," many writers have speculated that while print epistemology encouraged very stable notions of the self (for example, I am this body; I am male; I am white; I want to live in a nation that lets me be me), the Internet and the Web, along with digital communications, encourages a questioning and a loosening of categories of identity. Hence, because people take on all sorts of identities on the Web, they are encouraged to think about their own subjectivity as performative, as not based in nature. Jean Baudrillard, playing off of McLuhan's phrasing, put it this way: "McLuhan saw modern technologies as 'extensions of man.' We should see them, rather, as expulsions of man" (1996:35). For example, because one can perform both masculinity and femininity on the Web (or various ethnicities, class positions, or sexualities), there is a self-reflective realization that identity has always been performative, that we have never had completely stable "selves"—we only thought this was the case.

If we think about the relationship between ideology and the Web through the branch of media theory that probes the relationship between media as form and cultural consciousness, we are encouraged to find a mixture of the epistemologies and ontologies of print and rational cultures. As a result, we find logics that are more emotional, less rational; global and virtual rather than geographic and physical; performative selves rather than identities based on nature. Moreover, our reality becomes less "real" and more what Jean Baudrillard (1988) would call "hyperreal"—our understanding of every activity is already mediated through our having witnessed it on multiple occasions, already mediated through multiple and various representations and understandings. Our world becomes a world of simulations, a world that is already understood through the ways we have already seen it, the ways we have experienced it on-screen. Our activities have already been completed, our food already eaten, our sex already performed. "The real" is consistently compared and understood through the hyperreal and our own senses of self are understood as having already been performed elsewhere and simply reproduced again in our actions.

Of course, I should emphasize that these transitions in meanings, in ideology, are based in theoretical speculation. The way the Web actually does alter or change the way we think about self and others will clearly differ from the theoretical arguments I have described. However, while we may not be able to understand precisely how ideology is shaped and altered by changes in dominant modes of communication, it is clear that the dominant means of communication at any historical moment do alter what we think and how we think it, regardless of media content, regardless of cornflakes and Cadillacs. As students of the Web—all of us—it is imperative that we take our speculations seriously.

The relationship between ideology and the World Wide Web, like the relationship between ideology and any form of communication or social system, is a rich and complicated one. In this chapter, I've attempted to suggest that there are at least three ways in which ideology and the Web intersect. First, in the many ways the Web is configured within conversations and public argument—such rhetorical positions clearly work in the interests of dominant ideology. Second, in the ways that the "content" on the Web is itself shaped by ideological concerns on the dominant cultural level. Third, in the relationship between the Web as "form" and the types of knowledge and consciousness it encourages. Finally, while it is clear that the Web may bring—in fact, has already brought—changes in thought and consciousness, as students of the Web's influence, one of our most important tasks is to continue to question and critique these changes.

NOTES

1. Read Walter Ong's classic text *Orality and Literacy* (1982) for a summary of the differences between oral and print epistemologies. Also, see Ronald Deibert's more recent *Parchment, Printing, and Hypermedia* (1997) for a discussion of these changes on social and political networks from oral cultures through digital cultures.

Chapter 9

Performance

Dawn Dietrich

> There is a performative power in language acts that some users are quick to dismiss, but which raises a host of issues regarding our perceptions of reality, ourselves, and the communities to which we belong, both on-line and in the "real" world.

Each time I teach my course "Virtual (Real)ities: Literature, Technology, and Gender," I hear interesting stories about students' experiences in cyberspace. Whether it is the heterosexual male who engages in a titillating exchange with a female, only to find out that *she* is male (or so she claims at the end of the conversation), or whether it is the female student who confides that she masquerades as a male on-line in order to avoid sexual harassment, contemporary students are aware of the "performative" freedoms and liabilities inherent in computer-mediated communication. Yet when students are asked to describe the meaning of "performance," they are still likely to associate the term more conventionally with the theater or performance artists, not with their own conduct or that of others on the Web.

It is clear that our understanding of what constitutes a performance is changing in a postmodern context. Notions of "live" performance and theatrical "embodiment" are undergoing radical change in a cultural context where speech is considered a "performative" act, and the live body has become conflated with its "virtual" representations. This chapter explores the contextualization of performance and performativity within a "posthuman" framework, or what Scott

Bukatman (1993) has defined as the new "terminal identity": the human-machine interface. For, as machines and information systems evolve, replicating human processes and actions, our understanding of agency is being transformed, and with it notions of human subjectivity and identity. (See "Identity," this volume) It comes as no surprise that many of these transformations are emerging through performance texts enacted on the World Wide Web.

To begin the discussion, it is necessary to identify the kind of transformation that has taken place as "live" performance has merged with visual media, and theorists have emphasized the "performative" dimension of language acts, both in terms of face-to-face discourse as well as computer-mediated communication. Performance discourse has undergone tremendous change since the 1970s, with a strained relationship emerging between conventional notions of theater and drama and the newer discipline of performance studies.[1] While theatrical performance, emerging from the disciplines of dramatic and literary studies, has come to be associated with textual authority, illusionism, and the canonical actor, performance studies has emerged from cultural studies paradigms to signify what is often perceived as a nontheatrical, nonscripted type of performance *act* (Diamond 1996:3). In short, performance studies has adopted the *metaphor of performance* to create a paradigm of basic human interaction that manifests itself in actions as diverse as rituals, ceremonies, scripted behavior, and gender roles. The *idea* of "performance" has proven to be such a powerful trope that many scholars and theorists now view theatrical drama as a derivative mode of performance studies itself.

To differentiate the newer discipline of performance studies from theater and drama studies, the term "performativity" has been assigned to describe performative "acts" freed from theatrical conventions and traditions. In large part, the term designates the range of verbal and gestural signs that constitute various performative languages: languages which don't merely describe, but appear *to enact change or to cause things to happen by their utterative or gestural force.* Drawing on speech act theory, the performative is no longer located solely in the interface of the material world with the performer's body, but operates as part of a larger understanding of the performative nature of representational systems, several of which I explore in the upcoming sections.[2]

Postmodern Calibrations: The Cultural Geography
of the Machine

The ongoing debate between "performance" and "performativity" plays itself out in interesting ways on the World Wide Web. On some sites, for instance, electronic technologies translate an actual performance into digitized images, portraying a "live" act through cyberspatial media. However, because the conventional notion of "performance" relates to live theatrical performance, as loosely signified by embodied "actors" and dramatic conventions, Web-mediated performance is always, already seen as a substitute for the "real" performance. As such, it becomes a devalued term within patriarchal culture, aligned with the feminine in terms of gender, the nonoriginary in terms of myths of presence.

Such ambivalent use of the Web is embodied in the Survival Research Laboratories site located at www.srl.org. Survival Research Laboratories is a performance group devoted to constructing "autonomous" machines, which produce their own mechanized performances at gatherings where human beings are present only as audience or operators (Pauline 1994:287). Mark Pauline (1995), the founder of Survival Research Laboratories, describes the performance group as "an organization of creative technicians, dedicated to re-directing the techniques, tools, and tenets of industry, science, and the military away from their typical manifestation in practicality, product or warfare" (Official Web Site Statement). The group has created teleoperated weaponry and robotics, such as giant insectlike walking machines, shock-wave cannons, and mechanical exoskeletons, designed to be driven by small rodents. These "machines" take on a surreal presence as they menace one another or audience members in ritualized spectacles characterized by flames, explosions, and sonic booms. As a kind of Theater of Operations, each performance is rendered unpredictable when the machines are set in motion and left to run of their own "free will"; at the same time, the machines are oddly beautiful, and even elegant in their artful design. Although banned in many U. S. cities, Survival Research Laboratories attracts audience members in droves, with spectators occasionally experiencing hearing loss, abrasions, burns, and broken bones in their chance encounters with these postmodern "performers."

Survival Research Laboratories is an interesting project to study in terms of performance on the Web because the group's initial impulse was to take performance back to its ritualistic roots by concentrating *live* experience until it unfolded as the spectacular. This involves a notion of performance that consciously moves *away* from the reproduction of virtual technologies toward a cathartic event presumably "outside" of copies, transmissions, and representations of technological culture (Bell 1997:3). In other words, it is an understanding of performance that locates *presence* in the live event. Yet, because Survival Research Laboratories uses technological forms (radio- and computer-operated remote controls, for instance) to critique the spectacle of postmodern culture, a negotiation with contemporary imaging technologies is unavoidable.

As an example, Survival Research Laboratories has set up a Web site and offered wireless audio-video broadcasting of several of its performances. This would seem to contradict the group's mission to engage audiences in the "spectacular real," as the digitized images offer quite another experience. And yet, only a few explanations have been offered as to why the group made this choice, and none seem sufficiently convincing. Interestingly, the lack of official explanations has opened up a gap for fans to speculate about this decision on the World Wide Web. Many fans have felt that in order not to appear to contradict the primary experience of a Survival Research Laboratories performance, some response had to be offered with regard to the media and its role in translating the performances across cyberspatial planes. One Survival Research Laboratories fan (1995) offered these thoughts on the live audio-video broadcast of Survival Research Laboratories' "Sickening Episodes of Devastation and Pleasure":

> Sure, the Web isn't the best way to witness the robotic chaos unleashed by Survival Research Laboratories (SRL). For one thing, an actual SRL "art" performance—in which fearsome automata threaten to turn against the squishy-skinned, defenseless audience—is about as disturbing and visceral as an earthquake at epicenter. The machines—constructed from surplus military parts, jet engines, and other industrial detritus—walk, grind, spit flame, shoot bullets, scream, and actually cause your flesh to vibrate. Sometimes they explode in a shower of shrapnel, injuring hapless bystanders. There's little chance of your PC or Mac combusting in your face while you browse the SRL Web page, but since mad genius Mark Pauline has trouble finding venues willing to host his "Sickening Episodes of Widespread Devastation Accompanied by Sensations of

Pleasurable Excitement," the Web may be the only place to encounter the San Francisco-based performance art troupe. MPEG videos give a taste of the power of an SRL event—especially the scared-stiff expressions of onlookers, their hair actually standing on end. Pauline (who sacrificed a thumb to his art and, true to his machinist aesthetic, had a toe transplanted to his hand) has loaded the site with amazing sounds and sights, including a jumbo close-up of a jagged wound on his thigh that had to be stitched up like a baseball. (cnet.com)

According to this fan's (1995) description, the virtualized performance reads like a parody of a Survival Research Laboratories performance, with viewers watching "the scared-stiff expressions of digitized onlookers, their hair actually standing on end." The writer acknowledges that no one could possibly mistake the virtual performance for the "real" thing. It is also implied that the virtualized representation is only a second-best substitute for the one, true (originary) performance. The fan concedes that the representational images may be necessary in this instance (since Pauline has had trouble obtaining permits for his machine performances from police and fire marshals), but insinuates that they are clearly "inauthentic." There is a palpable tension between the writer's acknowledgment of the necessity for the reproductive images and his/her resentment about their "appropriation" of a performance at once "true," "live," and "masculine."

What the fan *doesn't* acknowledge in the Web performance is the translation of one ideological moment into another in the process. The co-optation of Survival Research Laboratories' industrial machines by cybertechnologies stands as a defining aesthetic of the late twentieth century—a shift in the ideology of technology. Even a performance "authenticated" by its physical presence stands to be subsumed by the larger imaging capabilities of the new information technologies. Hence, an uneasy alliance is struck: Survival Research Laboratories is reduced to an image, but allowed a social space in which to present its performance. Cyberviewers cannot claim they have attended a "live" performance, but more of them can witness the spectacle on a purely representational level.

I believe that this example speaks to more than just a specific Web performance; that is, it begins to address some of the social changes that are taking place as human and machine cultures become increasingly interdependent. In this case, "performance" becomes a trope with which to explore the cyborg nature of humankind, especially the fears and anxieties that get raised regarding electronic technologies, gender, and identity.

Regarding the co-optation of Survival Research Laboratories, I see a negotiation happening that pits a nostalgic longing for the visible, "masculine" machine (born of the Industrial Age in the United States) against a fear of the more invisible, "feminized" technologies of cyberspace, cyborg manifestations, and intraorganic processes, all of which represent an intrusion into the "text" of the body. In short, ideologies of gender influence the perception of the Web as a substitute for something more "real." (See "Ideology," this volume.)

In the first place, machines epitomize the shifting boundary between the natural and the cultural, creating anxiety in many people about what constitutes "a person" or what counts as (human) agency. The nature-culture binary has particularly come under attack in the late twentieth century with the advent of computer technologies and artificial life forms; and the ambiguity of the human-machine interface has led to a kind of nostalgia for gender differentiation and absolute forms of self-identity. At a time of tremendous uncertainty about the body and its representations, there is an intensified focus on machines and their relationship to the human body. Cultural critic Claudia Springer writes, "Mechanical objects have been imbued with male and/or female characteristics for centuries; consequently, representations of machines long have been used to express ideas about sexual identity and gender roles" (1996:9).

Survival Research Laboratories draws on an older military-industrial paradigm generated by machinic, manufacturing, and military uses of technology. From the dynamo to the turbine, industrial machines ushered in a highly technological twentieth century, which required a reevaluation of human agency as machines were able to duplicate and even improve upon human labor. Industrial machines tended to be utilitarian in function, daunting in size, and extremely noisy. With some of the more sophisticated designs, the machines had a three-dimensional presence which allowed them to move through space in a way that resembled human physiology and form; and some machines were even anthropomorphized to resemble a human figure, as with the automaton or the robot. Though industrial machines replicated human work, which led to unemployment in certain sectors of the population, the prevailing representation of the worker depicted him or her as "freed" from the burden of material labor.

Hence, the monstrous machines were strategically marketed as industrious robots skilled at accomplishing work that was dangerous, repetitive, or simply boring. Rather than creating a threatening presence, the large machines often elicited pride among Americans who saw them as tokens of industrial modernity, speed, and productivity. In time, the machines also became powerful metaphors for masculine virility and strength, in part because of the "violent desires incited by the systemic, the repetitive, and the automatistic" (Seltzer 1992:19).

In contrast to the Industrial Age, the late twentieth century ushered in an era of miniaturized circuits, teleoperated machinery, and electronic computers. Of course, different metaphors are required to understand our relationship to these new machines, which tend to generate capital through reproduction, virtual models, and simulations. Fredric Jameson (1991) notes that "the technology of our own moment no longer possesses [the] same capacity for representation." He uses the example of the computer console, "whose outer shell has no emblematic or visual power," or the television "which articulates nothing . . . , carrying its flattened image surface within itself" (1991:37).

Because information technologies, including the Web, do not signify as instruments of *visible power* within patriarchal culture, they are often read as "female," so that fears about the "natural" and the "cultural" body get displaced onto the woman's body. In effect, the female becomes collapsed with the postmodern machine, generating anxiety about gender differentiation and identity, and fears about bodily colonization. Claudia Springer (1996) explores the connections between femininity, desire, and machine culture in her book *Electronic Eros: Bodies and Desire in the Postindustrial Age*. Though she acknowledges that computers can have an ambiguous relationship to gender, most of her discussion centers on the view that representations of computers are gendered female in the popular imagination because of their "small size, fluid and quiet functioning, and the ability to absorb the user's ego in an emphatic bond" (1996:9). This view is often echoed in cultural studies of cyberspace as well. For example, technocritic Allucquere Roseanne Stone states, "to become the cyborg, is to put on the seductive and dangerous cybernetic space like a garment, is to put on the female" (1991:109). In addition, feminist critic Anne Balsamo argues that "Certain technologies. . . [are] ideologically shaped by the operation of gender interests and, consequently . . . for example, serve to reinforce traditional gendered patterns of power and authority" (1996:10). These feminist critics are referring to traditional gender binaries in order to define this postmodern moment. By elucidating patriarchal projections and fantasies regarding cybertechnologies, they hope to draw attention to the potential these machines have to deconstruct rather than reinforce such gender categories.[3] (See "Gender," this volume.)

In a "masculinist" culture so mediated by "feminine" cybertechnologies, the physical assault provided by Survival Research Laboratories provides an adrenaline rush for a postmodern fringe interested in producing and sustaining the ideological space of the autonomous machine. Michael Bell (1997) identifies this trend in his essay, "Functions of Performance in Technological-Spectacular Culture." He writes, "As cyberculture continues to replace physical contact with virtual contact and experience with semiotics, performance could be employed more and more in the service of bringing human beings back into contact with experiences of the physical body and memories of instinct" (1997:7). With a nostalgia firmly rooted in the physical production of capital and goods, the masculine machine represents patriarchal culture at the height of its productive imperialism.

To the contrary, advertising languages and simulacra project the "feminine hyperreal," an environment in which we move through the simulated within contemporary culture. J. G. Ballard (1970) noted in an early interview, "If anything is to have meaning for us in this postmodern . . . [moment], it must take place in terms of the values and experiences of the media landscape" (Barber 1970:57). In order for Survival Research Laboratories to create meaning within this cultural context, they must embrace *and* resist the cultural tendency toward "surface" and away from "depth"—the tendency of the cultural screen to co-opt the "real" for the representation, the image for the "experience." In this nostalgic social space, there is a fascination with performance on the World Wide Web, but it is still seen as *a substitute for something else.* Put simply, a traditional notion of performance underlies Survival Research Laboratories' work, rendering the equivocal nature of "performativity" fearsome and untrustworthy to the group and many of its fans.

This uneasy alliance between "productive" industrial machines and "reproductive" cybertechnologies is borne out in an odd personal detail: Mark Pauline's disfigured hand. Destroyed when he was attempting to build a rocket engine, Pauline's right hand has been sewn together with three of his toes providing finger-like digits. Pauline (1994) acknowledges,

> My damaged right hand enjoys a respectable notoriety. For instance, a recent article that appeared in *TIME* magazine regarding the *Cyberpunk* phenomenon devoted more copy to my hand than it did to SRL activities. I have weathered a variety of interesting reactions to this appendage over the years, from simple handshake-repulsion, to cultivated indifference, to ridiculous suggestions of its extraordinary abilities. Certainly, it has earned the right (by ordeal if nothing else) to at least some of this attention. To me it remains a testament to the distinction that ought to be made between a reasonable infatuation with the merely hazardous and senseless flirtation with self-destruction. (1994:293)

Pauline is correct when he recognizes that his wounded hand "speaks" to postmodern enthusiasts, but it does not necessarily serve as a precautionary sign. Rather, Pauline's damaged hand signifies the difference between attending the performance of real, masculine machines and watching reproduced images of them. His scars are a testament to the mortal body, to the pre-telematic, male body that threatens to "disappear" in this postmodern moment. Audience members are drawn to the "perverse" flesh because it signifies the latent desire to merge with electronic technologies; because it bears the sign of the postmodern machine that both creates and destroys. In other words, bearing witness to the narrative of the wounded body inspires a nostalgic faith in the flesh, a retro-empathy that links individuals together in a defense against a virtual age that threatens to dissolve the physical body. Paul Virilio writes, "With [technological] acceleration there is no more here and there only mental confusion of near and far, present and future, real and unreal—a mix of history, stories, and the hallucination utopia of communication and technologies" (1995:35).

In this case Mark Pauline's body registers the transition of one ideological moment giving way to another—from the autonomous Industrial Age robot to the human-machine interface—a radical departure marked by an eruption of violent posthuman narratives. Because Survival Research Laboratories grounds the "real" in the performative body-machine, patriarchal gender construction guides the sense of the Web as a "substitute," a surrogate for this primary, masculine event. Undoubtedly, the potential for greater experimentation lies with the newer "performativity" and those individuals interested in exploring human subjectivity, identity, and gender on new frontiers. (See "Identity" and "Gender," this volume.)

Performing the Wor(l)d

Moving toward the "feminine" hyperreal or the human-machine interface, "performance" comes to be understood differently in the context of interactive avatars (self-identified cyberspatial personas) and three-dimensional Web environments. Here, the performative drops away from the purely physical to become embedded in the metaphorical, namely language, or language systems. To provide a sense of historical perspective on this newer "performativity," I will review the now infamous case of the "cyber-rape" that took place within the text-based LambdaMOO, a database maintained by Xerox Corporation for research purposes.[4]

In this MOO, designed to give users the feel of moving through three-dimensional space, a user identified as "Mr. Bungle" (a "fat, oleaginous, Bisquick-faced clown dressed in cum-stained harlequin garb and girdled with a mistletoe-and-hemlock belt whose buckle bore the quaint inscription 'KISS ME UNDER THIS BITCH!'") forced other participants to gratify him with sexual favors and to commit violent acts against one another (Dibbell 1994:239).[5] For example, it was reported that Mr. Bungle forced a participant known as "legba" "to sexually service him in more or less conventional ways," then eat her own pubic hair; and he caused a character named "Starsinger" to violate herself with a kitchen knife (1994:239). Bungle accomplished these acts by manipulating the "voodoo" doll, a subprogram that could attribute actions to characters that did not originate with the users. Though he was immediately ejected from the room, he was still able to manipulate "legba" into "unwanted liaisons with other individuals" because she remained in proximity to the voodoo doll (1994:239). Needless to say, the participants of LambdaMOO were offended by Bungle's aggressive behavior and felt it violated a trust they had built as a virtual community. They set about discussing ways to punish or discipline the user known as "Mr. Bungle." What ensued was a fascinating exploration of the nature of this cybercrime and its relation to "performativity," or the power of language to "perform" acts.

Like the digitized performances of Survival Research Laboratories, the Bungle rape signifies a paradigm shift, but one of a different nature; drawing on notions of the performativity of language, derived from speech act theory, this case questioned the legitimacy of *interpreting words as deeds within Web contexts*. Since the commands typed into a computer are a kind of speech that makes things happen, much as the marriage vow is a ritualistic deed, the question becomes, Should Websites afford words the kind of legal power and responsibility that only *actions* have in the "real" world? In other words, is the conflation of speech and act inevitable in a computer-mediated context? If so, should writing be viewed as a performative act in its own right? Of course, the most frightening aspect of such a suggestion is the threat it poses to our freedoms of expression, including First Amendment rights. Yet, advocates of such cyberlaws argue that language can no longer be separated from the realm of action, especially in the context of computer-mediated communication.

To return to the Bungle case, the culprit could not be stopped until Zippy, a long-time participant in the LambdaMOO, shot Bungle with a magical gun designed to incarcerate him in a cage. But a short time later, another character in the MOO let Bungle out without realizing the extent of his pernicious deeds. Bungle wasn't positively dealt with until "legba" called for his "toading," a death act that brings about the annihilation of both the character and the user account. After much consideration, the cybercommunity agreed with her. The participants then petitioned one of the master programmers of LambdaMOO to carry out the "toading" and "eliminate" Bungle. After some administrative soul-searching (the programmers had sworn themselves to a policy of "laissez-faire"), one of the programmers quietly performed the act. Now when users typed the @who command on "Bungle," they received the message that "Mr. Bungle was not the name of any player." Yet, months later when an eccentric character named Dr. Jest emerged from within the community, "stuffing fellow players into a jar containing a tiny simulacrum of a certain deceased rapist," users still couldn't be sure that "Bungle" was really gone (Dibbell 1994:254). Many feared that he had signed on as a new user. Julian Dibbell (1994) describes the confusion between the "real" and the "virtual" acts of Bungle and the user he represented:

while a certain tension invariably buzzes in the gap between the hard, prosaic RL [real life] facts and their more fluid, dreamy VR [virtual reality] counterparts, the dissonance in the Bungle case is striking. No hideous clowns or trickster spirits appear in the RL version of the incident, no voodoo dolls or wizard guns, indeed no rape at all as any RL court of law has yet defined it. The actors in the drama were university students for the most part, and they sat rather undramatically before computer screens the entire time, their only actions a spidery flitting of fingers across standard QWERTY keyboards. No bodies touched. Whatever physical interaction occurred consisted of a mingling of electronic signals sent from sites spread out between New York City and Sydney, Australia. Those signals met in LambdaMOO, certainly, just as the hideous clown and the living room party did, but what was LambdaMOO after all? Not an enchanted mansion or anything of the sort—just a middlingly complex database . . . open to public access via the Internet. (1994:240)

So, was a crime committed? Because the LambdaMOO program was written to correspond to the laws of the physical world (users had to find doors to exit and enter, for instance, and could only "see" other players in the immediate vicinity), it provided some illusion of "presence," but in real life logistics, the only thing that moved was the written script of the individual users. After the event, Dibbell records, the character known as "legba" responded to the Bungle "rape" on a mailing list called *social issues:

> mostly I tend to think that restrictive measures around here cause more trouble than they prevent. But I also think that Mr. Bungle was being a vicious, vile fuckhead, and I . . . want his sorry ass scattered from #17 to the Cinder Pile. I'm not calling for policies, trials, or better jails. I'm not sure what I'm calling for. Virtual castration, if I could manage it. Mostly, [this type of thing] doesn't happen here. Mostly, perhaps, I thought it wouldn't happen to me. Mostly, I trust people to conduct themselves with some veneer of civility. Mostly, I want his ass. (1994:242)

Julian Dibbell spoke to the woman in Seattle who had created the avatar "legba." She confided to him that the actions of Bungle caused her tremendous real life trauma. The emotional power of the violent text was not something she could ignore, and there was no mistaking the gendered nature of the hateful "crime." Yet, Dibbell argues, the "reality" of the event was neither "here" nor "there." Other critics put it more strongly, arguing that the "crime" was not a "rape" and that calling it that trivialized the anguish of "real" victims who had been physically violated. Dibbell writes,

> Where virtual reality and its conventions would have us believe that legba and Starsinger were brutally raped in their own living room, here was the victim legba scolding Mr. Bungle for a breach of "civility." Where real life, on the other hand, insists the incident was only an episode in a free-form version of Dungeons and Dragons, confined to the realm of the symbolic and at no point threatening any player's life, limb, or material well-being, here now was the player legba issuing aggrieved and heartfelt calls for Mr. Bungle's dismemberment. Ludicrously excessive by RL's lights, woefully understated by VR's, the tone of legba's response made sense only in the buzzing, dissonant gap between them. (1994:243)

Perhaps the only conclusion that can be drawn from this experience is that cyberspatial exchanges are neither "here" nor "there," but exist somewhere between the two directional planes in the murky space of the Web. Wherever they exist and however they are defined, many users find the exchanges emotionally meaningful. Performative acts bring about consequences, despite anonymity or pseudonymity, especially when these "acts" involve sex, violence, or self-representation. In this case, for example, gendered behavior was very much a part of the anonymous exchange, for the "disembodied" acts performed by Bungle mimicked the kinds of wholesale violence directed at women in "real" world contexts. In short, there is a performative power in language acts that some users are quick to dismiss, but which raises a host of issues regarding our perceptions of reality, ourselves, and the communities to which we belong, both on-line and in the "real" world.

The LambdaMOO incident differs from the Survival Research Laboratories example to the extent that LambdaMOO participants were self-conscious about gender and sensitive to the ways in which gender conventions, including abuses, get acted out on the Web. In the Bungle case, the egregious act was too close to the kind of physical violence directed against women in the real world for the participants to ignore its ramifications. Rather than remain impervious to the effects of gender construction within a patriarchal context, the LambdaMOO community dealt with the situation by negotiating their differences openly and recognizing the role gender plays in the construction of on-line personalities and behavior.

This kind of self-awareness is paramount if we are going to shape electronic technologies to meet the needs of a diverse and multicultural population. The various debates instigated by the Bungle "rape" have illuminated some of the discussions that point us toward a future where we will interact more and more frequently in electronic contexts. It is safe to say that on-line worlds involve socialization rituals and enactments—that the performative is always embedded within the social, within our language acts—and as such can never be thought of as "risk-free." These are the realizations that have taken the traditional notion of "performance" in new directions, namely, toward the postmodern "performative."

Virtual (Real)ity

Web "enactments" or performances become even more seductive when words are embellished with graphics and audio capability. The more sophisticated computer environments now allow users to manipulate graphics-based avatars, often interacting with various forms of Artificial Intelligence. Stanford's Virtual Theater site, part of the Adaptive Intelligent Systems (AIS) project, is one of the more interesting experiments involving interactive gaming on the Web.[6] Ironically, the designers have structured a multimedia environment in which users can enact all the roles associated with producing and staging a conventional play in the "real" world. For example, the user can fulfill the role of playwright, set designer, or actor. The roles the user does not enact are played by "Intelligent agents" who bring "lifelike" qualities to their performances, including improvisational acting techniques. Actors in the production respond to an automated stage manager as well as instructions from on-line users, so that the site offers interesting opportunities for collaboration with Artificial Intelligence.

Once we have arrived at on-line exchanges with Artificial Intelligence, it does not require a great leap to imagine mass-produced virtual reality systems and technologies, whereby users don head, hand, and/or body gear and physically engage their whole bodies in computer-mediated landscapes or environments. At this time it is apparent that virtual reality applications are the evolutionary successors to interactive Websites, though such systems are still in the early phases of development and are generally prohibitively expensive.

However, since the virtual future looms immanently upon the horizon, I will look at some of the performative issues inherent in full body immersion in electronic worlds. To begin I will consider the place that a project like Placeholder occupies as a virtual reality installment *and* an interactive Web site. Produced by Interval Research Corporation and the Banff Centre, and directed by Brenda Laurel and Rachel Strickland, this project undertook an ambitious multimedia experiment in order to further our understanding of human-machine interactions and to experiment with notions of performativity on the Web. Basically, the researchers use the Web to document their virtual reality project; users can find design sketches, photos, computer models, postproduction publications, and even video framegrabs from participants' helmets on the Web site. Placeholder, the virtual reality project, offers an interesting contrast to Survival Research Laboratories and LambdaMOO because it brings the physical back to the Web, *but through the context of performativity*. In this instance, there is a focus on performativity, so that computer-mediated communication is not utilized as a substitute for something else. Rather, *it creates action*, much as language does in speech-act theory. The computer-mediated environment becomes a social space where we can begin to rethink issues of identity and subjectivity, where we can begin to transform our constructed notions of what it means to be human.

In essence, Laurel and Strickland have created a new paradigm for narrative action within virtual environments. Their link of electronic technologies and narrative form signifies their interest in the performative, as does their realization that *language creates action and informs subjectivity*. Before exploring the role language plays in their virtual reality project, however, I will describe the physical features of the project. The geography of Placeholder was derived from three actual locations in the Banff National Park—a cave, a waterfall, and a formation of weathered rock near a riverbed. One reason Laurel and Strickland's work is notable is because they successfully created three-dimensional videographic imagery, spatialized sounds and voices, and user embodiment in the form of "petroglyphic spirit animals." Physically remote users wearing head-mounted displays can enter any of the three worlds, viewing and touching a composite landscape. Guided by a disembodied "Voice of the Goddess," users can engage in conversation, explore the virtual world by interacting with it, and create and record their own narrative account of the experience.

Laurel and Strickland did not choose the actual park sites in order to achieve a high degree of sensory realism, even though their technological accomplishments are notable. Rather, the two researchers were interested in capturing a real sense of "place." For Laurel and Strickland, this involved understanding "place" as a composite production of human perception and intelligence, as well as landscape features. They were interested in the ways that "place" could be experienced and marked through narrative activity, intimating that places are created through language. The two researchers began asking themselves difficult questions: How is any one place organized spatially? How does one know "where" one is? How can place be captured simultaneously rather than sequentially, using a time-based medium like video? And what are the virtual equivalents of footprints, graffiti, and shadows? (Strickland 1994:1–5) The exploratory answers to these questions—along with the support of Crystal River Engineering and technicians Rob Tow, Michael Naimark, and John Harrison—helped Laurel and Strickland begin to shape the technologies and software that would construct their virtual world.

Despite the incredible technical accomplishments of the two researchers and their production crew, it is important to recognize that Placeholder is as much a social inquiry into the nature of human-machine interactions as it is an experiment with cutting-edge technologies. In many ways the researchers set up challenges that were far more sophisticated than working out a simple design for human-machine interface. There was that part of the project, certainly—negotiations were ongoing for working out glitches and dealing with error-prone computers and recording devices—but the experiment amounted to more than that in the long run.[7] For example, when looking back upon the whole project which was never developed to its full potential, Laurel acknowledged the many technical shortcomings (mostly due to time factors or lack of resources), but felt that overall they had succeeded because the participants had been invited to *produce* content by constructing meanings. More to the point, she believed that she and her team of technicians had created an interface that allowed users to experience the pleasure of embodied imagination (Laurel and Tow 1994:10).

To create a project that went further than most virtual reality experiments, Laurel and Strickland put the physical body back into the computer-mediated environment. They felt that the absence of haptic affordances (devices that give the bodily sensation of touch) in virtual reality interfaces had led to a dangerous sense of incorporeality, manifested in popular claims that the physical body, including gendered identities and material constraints, could be "left behind" in cyberspace. They wanted to put physical "action" back into the experience so that participants could "have" or "sense" a virtual body. This involved reexamining techniques that had become conventions in virtual reality research, such as the use of formal gestures to signify various meanings within virtual contexts. Laurel and Strickland wanted their interface to be imperceptible. They wanted to achieve a "naturalness" in terms of mobility and sensation, a coherence between vision and audition (Laurel and Tow 1994:9).

At the same time, and perhaps paradoxically, they were interested in challenging "naturalized" gender ideologies. One of the most interesting techniques they implemented was an identity-bending subprogram intended to get participants to experience place through an(other's) perception. In this instance, the researchers created "smart critters" with which participants could merge by joining their head to the creature's body. Once joined, the critter not only served as a graphics-based avatar for the user, but also dramatically altered the user's behavior by offering a novel type of nonhuman embodiment, including the acquisition of a different voice, perceptual characteristics, and means of locomotion. The researchers hoped that by foregrounding "difference," users would come to recognize the idiosyncratic ways in which they "constructed" both place and identity. Laurel emphasized that one of the most valuable outcomes of the project was the record left behind of how individuals reacted to the *"deconstruction" of their bodies in the realm of the senses* (Laurel, Strickland, and Tow 1994:12).[8]

This type of experimentation differs markedly from the ways in which Survival Research Laboratories nostalgically reinscribed the body-machine in their protorealist performances or LambdaMOO created language-based identities within Web contexts. Both Laurel and Strickland recognized the social and cultural implications inherent in reconstructing the virtual body—and with it patriarchal gender norms. This does not mean they believed traditional gender norms would fall away in their computer-mediated context, but that some effort was needed to destabilize the "normalizing" effects of such learned behavior.

In another phase of the project, Laurel and Strickland imaginatively explored landscape and its relation to performativity through the traces people leave behind in marking a place: their footsteps, shadows, and graffiti (Strickland 1994:3–4). The two researchers recognized their virtual landscape as something obviously shaped by visual representation techniques (panoramic surrounds and virtual relief-projection of camera-originated imagery, for instance), but they also acknowledged the role the participants' imagination played. They wanted to create a physical means by which individuals could leave behind their "marks," their perceptions of the three-dimensional environment, in order to interact and collaborate with one another in the creation of this narrative region. To accomplish this task, they created a technology which they called "voiceholders." "Voiceholders" appeared as rocks throughout the landscape, but functioned as a kind of audio-graffiti. Depending on their signification (closed or opened eyes and mouth), users could enter in their own recorded message or listen to the messages of others. In this way, the journey became a journey through language and verbal expression as well as digitized images, so that the "voices" of the participants were an integral part of the Placeholder experience.

Finally, Placeholder was about destabilizing binaries—between body and machine, sound and image, body and mind. It offered the individuals the chance to find their bodies (both real and virtual) in a new narrative region, a landscape of mind and imagination, but also one of strikingly real "physical" sensations. This return to the physical was enacted through performative gestures, which challenged traditional notions of subjectivity and identity. Where these kinds of new experiences will take us is hard to say at the present moment. But they promise the creation of new types of exchanges, different environments, and, by necessity, adapted subjects. It does not seem too great an exaggeration to suggest that new worlds are indeed being mapped out, imagined, and made real in the course of the users' engagement.

The interactive examples described in this chapter contextualize performance within a posthuman framework—what we might call our "terminal identity"—in postmodern terms. As machines and communications systems replicate human agency and as human beings assume disembodied identities, the boundaries which once demarcated the human from the machine and the "natural" from the "unnatural" are made more obscure. These computer-mediated texts articulate posthuman narratives which radically challenge not only our notions of performance, but those of subjectivity and identity as well. We are being made to imagine various subjectivities which may or may not include actual, physical embodiment. At the same time, imaging technologies and televisual reproductions are relaying live performances through screening contexts. Our words can now have the import of actions, and we may play with our own notions of identity in multiple-user contexts. Whatever claims may be made about "performance" or "performativity" on the Web, it is evident that these dramatic narratives operate as part of a larger "textual" exchange regarding our very subjective place in this postmodern moment.

NOTES

1. See W. B. Worthen's (1998) delineation of the key stages of this evolution. While I support his deconstruction of the binary opposition between "performance" and "performativity," my early examples attempt to understand how popular culture perceives the difference (if any) and acts upon it accordingly. This type of use involves a more generalized understanding of the two terms, but is not intended to oversimplify or negate Worthen's argument. I complicate the relationship between the two terms in my last example.

2. For an extended discussion of speech act theory, see J. L. Austin (1975).

3. For the most well-known feminist appropriation of the cyborg trope, see Donna Haraway (1991).

4. For a complete discussion of the LambdaMOO incident from one who participated in the community, I refer readers to Julian Dibbell (1994).

5. For readers unfamiliar with computer lingo, "MOO" is an acronym for "multi-oriented objects."

6. Locate the site at http://www-ksl.stanford.edu/projects/cait/index.html.

7. Read the post-production papers written by Brenda Laurel, Rachel Strickland, and Rob Low for their humorous tales recounting the foibles of working with new media. For example, there are interesting descriptions of working with "fields" of sound, rather than "points" of sound. (See Laurel's description of obtaining the waterfall sound effects, which required that Rob Low literally stand under the falls wearing a microphone protected by an un-lubricated condom!) There is also a very engaging discussion of the difficul-

ties inherent in creating the "different" perceptions of the smart critters as well as descriptions of how imprecise handwork had to accomplish delicate feats, such as camera positioning which could facilitate the wireframe design of the three-dimensional videographic output.

8. See the transcription of the voicemarks and the published interviews of users' experiences with Placeholder in "Post-Production Papers," located on the Web site.

Chapter 10

Hypertext

Matthew G. Kirschenbaum

Even the very word itself, "hypertext," seems to have
acquired an electric sheen, capturing the kinetic excitement of the Information Age, the bright neon riot reflected in the mirrorshade pages of Wired magazine.

Hypertext is a word with a wide Web of connotations and associations,
and this is fitting given its essential meaning. Typically, hypertext (or
"hypermedia," as it is called when images and sound are also involved)
is taken to mean electronic text organized as a nonsequential system of
links and destinations—these destinations have been variously called
"nodes," "lexias," "screens," "writing spaces," or, on the Web, "pages"
and "sites." Readers "follow" links (by clicking them) to create their
own "paths" or "trails" through the connected documents. Among
other things, this means that no two readers may read a hypertext in exactly the same way, and that the reading process is active and exploratory rather than passive and predetermined.

From this seemingly modest definition, hypertext has been celebrated as the technological realization of large-scale changes in
human thought and perception—nothing less than "a new relationship between thinking man and the sum of knowledge," as one early
visionary enthusiastically described it.[1] Today, hypertext is at the center of the postmillennial dream of a seamlessly integrated global network of information; indeed, Xanadu, one of the most elaborate hypertext systems ever devised (and never built), in the late 1960s, was
a remarkably prescient anticipation of certain aspects of the World

Wide Web. Science fiction writers have also done much to popularize hypertext, tantalizing readers with the promise of a universe of knowledge at their fingertips: digital encyclopedias and libraries, vast galaxies and constellations of information, virtual worlds without end, all woven together by the electronic threads of links, nodes, and paths. Even the very word "hypertext" seems to have acquired an electric sheen, capturing the kinetic excitement of the Information Age, the bright neon riot reflected in the mirrorshade pages of *Wired* magazine. Yet hypertext is also a technical term, with an important lineage in computer science disciplines like information retrieval, document encoding, and visualization; and of course, "hypertext" comprises one half of the acronym HTML, which has itself become a household word in recent years. (Also see "Multimedia" and "Narrative," this volume.)

So hypertext, despite its deceptively simple definition as nonlinear electronic writing, is many different things to many different people. Hypertext is both a text and a technology, but—since texts themselves are also technologies—there is no clear indication as to where the boundary lies between the two. Moreover, hypertext is also arguably both a genre and a medium. This raises questions such as whether every Web site is hypertext simply by virtue of its pedigree in HTML, or whether hypertext embodies something more—aesthetically, conceptually, or computationally—than just the mechanical processes of linking. This is typical of the kind of question that has occupied hypertext theorists in recent years, especially since the Web is often branded as a relatively poor and unimaginative realization of certain ideas pioneered by early hypertext developers. In what follows, I will be looking more closely at some current debates concerning hypertext, while paying particular attention to the Web, which is unquestionably the largest, the most popular, and socially, culturally, and economically speaking, the most *complex* hypertext system in existence.

How Old Is Hypertext?

There is no single answer to this question but there are many milestones. Hypertext is certainly older than the World Wide Web, and even on the Web it may be older than you think: HTML was originally drafted by a physicist named Tim Berners-Lee in 1990. At the time, he imagined it as nothing more than a convenient system that would allow scientists to use their computers to exchange their research with one another. Three years before that, however—three years before the Web was even conceived—the Association for Computing Machinery held the first of what was to become a series of annual international conferences on hypertext. In 1987, the same year as that inaugural hypertext conference, Apple introduced Hypercard, the first widespread hypertext authoring system for personal computers (it came preinstalled on all Macs); also in 1987, a writer named Michael Joyce began circulating on floppy disk the work widely regarded as the first hypertext novel, entitled *afternoon: a story* (*afternoon* would be released in a revised edition in 1990 by Eastgate Systems, who continue to publish Joyce's work to this day, together with that of a growing number of authors of electronic fiction, poetry, and nonfiction prose).

So hypertext certainly predates the Web, with the first functional hypertext systems emerging in the mid-1980s. The word "hypertext" itself is even older, dating back as far as 1965, when computer visionary Theodore ("Ted") Nelson gave a talk about something he called "hyper-text" to an audience at Vassar College, in New York. He described it as "a more flexible, more generalized, non-linear presentation of material on a particular subject."[2] But hypertext (as a concept, if not the specific word) is often traced back even further, to a 1945 article entitled "As We May Think" in *Atlantic Monthly* magazine by Vannevar Bush. In it, Bush, a prominent American scientist, proposed what was essentially an interactive desk (a workstation he called the "Memex") that would allow researchers to link together "trails" of microfilm—microfilm being the preeminent document storage technology of the day—in ways remarkably similar to the link structures now characteristic of electronic hypertext. Bush based his rationale for the Memex on the same grounds that are cited by today's hypertext developers: that it facilitated the kind of "associative thinking" that supposedly mirrors the mind's natural functions. But if we admit that the concept of hypertext is older than the word itself, then we can perhaps trace it back even further—to Argentine writer Jorge Luis Borge's 1941 story "The Garden of Forking Paths" which posits several alternative endings, or to Laurence Sterne's eighteenth-century antinovel *Tristram Shandy*, which deconstructed the linear narrative structures of prose fiction; or perhaps to the Talmud, a collection of glosses and interpretations of Jewish law and custom dating to the fifth century A.D. that has been densely annotated and cross-referenced by generations of rabbinical commentators. In fact, the question of whether "hypertext" must be presented electronically—in the environment of a computer—is central to current debates in hypertext theory.

Isn't Hypertext Just a Digital Footnote?

Hypertext developers have long recognized the parallels between electronic links and the footnotes in conventional printed texts. Footnotes are so commonplace that they are often taken for granted by readers—but in fact they are one of the most effective mechanisms we have for heightening the functionality of what Canadian writers Steve McCaffery and bpNichol (1992) have called "the book machine." Footnotes stratify the linear presentation of conventional prose. Typically an author has a reference or citation to include, or an additional point he or she wants to make. Providing that extra information on the spot, in the main body of the text, would be distracting and disruptive. The footnote, which is essentially an analog technology for displacing text on a page, serves to alert the reader and redirect his or her attention, while also leaving the reader free to ignore it if desired. All this is similar at some levels to the basic function of a hypertext link, but to equate hypertext with footnotes is unduly reductive.

First, there are many different kinds of hypertext links. On the Web, links have remained relatively crude devices, generally allowing a reader to access only one page at a time. As anyone who has used browsers such as Netscape or Internet Explorer will know, clicking a linked word or phrase initiates a process that loads a new page in their browser window (or else opens a second browser window). But we have already seen that hypertext as a concept is much older than the Web, and that functional hypertext systems had been implemented years before the Web came into existence. Many of these early systems included far more sophisticated linking capabilities: "one-to-many" linking, for example, where a single click might open several interrelated windows containing additional writing spaces as well as images and other material. (A hypertext system developed at Brown University called Intermedia was capable of such behavior as far back as 1985.) Likewise, Storyspace, a hypertext authoring system also released in the 1980s (and still in use today) implemented a feature called "guard fields," which cannot be duplicated on the Web without specialized scripting and programming: guard fields track a reader's progress through a hypertext, and control access to certain writing spaces based on those links which the reader has already visited. Some writing spaces may be altogether inaccessible unless the reader has followed certain necessary links as prerequisites; other spaces might have links that lead to different destinations depending upon the reader's prior history as tracked by the guard fields. While this scenario might seem restrictive or intrusive to readers accustomed to the surf and click navigation of the Web where there is instant access to anything anytime anywhere, guard fields can in fact facilitate richly structured hypertexts that present information in carefully controlled contexts—a kind of artificial intelligence that responds to the needs of an individual reader based on what he or she already knows. One-to-many linking and guard fields are both examples of important hypertext features that transcend the functionality of the footnote.

Perhaps most importantly, footnotes are still bound by the physical limitations of the book. If an author wants to reference an article in support of her argument, for example, the convention is to provide readers with the information they would need to look up the article for themselves. Because computers do not face the same physical limitations as books (which is *not* to say that they face no limitations at all—quite the contrary) the "footnote" could theoretically comprise the full text of the referenced article. Or the "footnote" could be a video clip of the author rebutting an anticipated objection to her main point (this would be an example of hypermedia). The radical potential of electronic hypertext begins to emerge from these examples, as do the limitations of defining hypertext strictly in relation to established textual technologies like footnotes, indices, and concordances.

Hypertext calls for new theories of textuality, new ways of thinking critically about the reading and writing process. Some theorists, authors, and designers have chosen to emphasize the experience of looking at hypertext in visual terms, encouraged by its maplike structures of links and nodes. Michael Joyce (1995) has famously stated: "Hypertext is, before anything else, a visual form." Jay David Bolter (1990), one of the codevelopers of Storyspace and an influential observer of new media, has characterized electronic writing as "topographic," meaning that reading is a fundamentally spatial experience: wandering the garden of forking paths that characterize the best hypertexts is an exploratory process.

Hypertext also demands new ways of thinking about the structures of texts. To return to the footnote, in print there is almost always a clear distinction between the main body of the text and the footnote, which is typically relegated to the back of the book or the margins of the page. But no such hierarchy need obtain in hypertext. How then can one visualize and understand the structure of a hypertext? This is a key problem that interface designers have worked to resolve. Storyspace, for example, includes a number of different options for visualizing hypertext structures, and there are also impressive visualization tools now being developed for the Web.

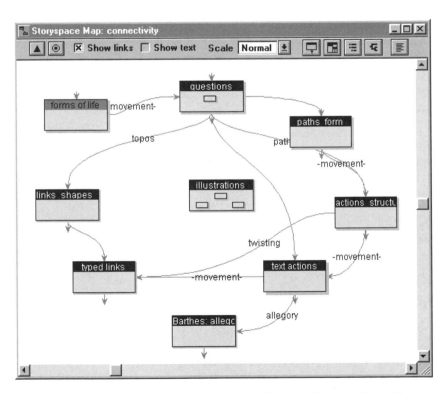

A typical Storyspace map view. Courtesy of Eastgate Systems. http://www .eastgate.com

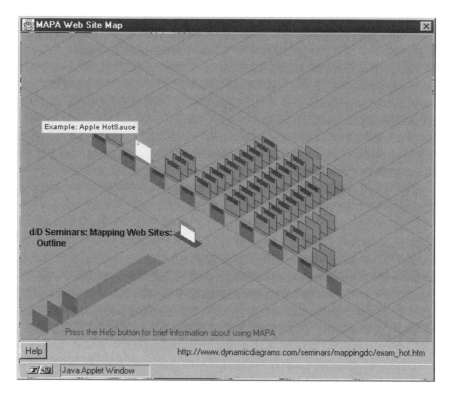

The "MAPA" applet for mapping Websites. Courtesy of Dynamic Diagrams. http://www.dynamicdiagrams.com

The different internal structures of a hypertext can also result in very different reading experiences. Michael Joyce (1995) usefully distinguishes between "constructive" hypertexts and those that are merely "exploratory." Constructive hypertexts, which are more ambitious, are those that involve the reader's active participation. Exploratory hypertexts are simply linked assemblages of materials, presented for the reader to passively browse. Long-time hypertext developers have frequently been critical of the Web because its conservative design traditions (note the preponderance of lists on many Web pages) and crude linking mechanisms typically encourage exploratory, rather than constructive, hypertexts. (If indeed the Web allows for functional hypertext at all—the hypermedia author and designer Stuart Moulthrop has wittily suggested that HTML should really stand for "HyperText More or Less.")

Texts and Hypertexts

To fully understand what hypertext is, we also need to address the question: what is *text*? The conventional wisdom is that texts are simply made up of words—sentences and paragraphs strung together to form some larger whole, be it a novel or a textbook or a technical manual. This is of course true to a point, but even a little bit of reflection should lead one to ask whether words and sentences and paragraphs are *all* that texts really are. Reading in fact depends upon the interaction of many different kinds of visual and linguistic elements. Consider a newspaper. The words and sentences that make up the linguistic content of the newspaper—that is, the "information" that we're presumably reading the paper for—are a part of the text, yes, but what about other components of the page? What about headlines and bylines? What about the section and page numbers printed across the top of each page (to facilitate navigation)? What about the many photographs and other kinds of graphics? What about advertisements? All these are part of the experience of reading a newspaper—certainly they are all part of the perceptual field that any reader of a modern newspaper encounters. Think of how much extra information is conveyed simply by the layout of the pages: stories near the top of a page are generally more important than stories further down, or below the fold; prominent stories are spread across multiple columns, and are given big, bold headlines; less important stories have smaller headlines, and are placed further back in the paper. Think about the effect achieved by the juxtaposition of multiple stories on a single newspaper page: does the surrounding content ever affect our reading of a given story? Think about the order in which one reads a newspaper: unlike a novel, where we typically begin at the beginning and read through to the final page of the final chapter, we read newspapers very differently: we skim them, even browse and surf them. If a story catches our interest—perhaps because of its striking headline or a prominent illustration—we may pause to read it through to the end. Or it might be continued on another page, and when we turn to that other page, relying on the printed section headings and page numbers to find our way, there might be a second story that engages our interest even further, and we may leave the first story aside to read the new one and then come back to the first story only later, or perhaps not at all. We may become distracted by an advertising supplement or a crossword puzzle or a comic strip. All this time we call what we are doing "reading," but cognitively we are doing much more than processing words.

It seems clear, then, that the "text" of a newspaper is made up of material beyond simple words and sentences. Now think about how one reads other kinds of printed matter: textbooks, catalogs, reference manuals, a volume of poetry, and so forth. In many cases, the reading habits associated with these texts closely resemble that of the newspaper: in fact, it may even be that the linear, tightly focused reading we associate with novels—beginning at the beginning and ending at the end, with no variation or distraction in between—is actually the exception rather than the rule.

Literary scholars know that some of our most compelling works and writers have been obsessed by the pliability of textual structures and narrative forms. Centuries ago, before the advent of the printing press, medieval monks illuminated manuscripts to enable letters to communicate graphically as well as semantically. Laurence Sterne broke most of the rules of traditional novel writing even before his eighteenth-century contemporaries had finished figuring them out. William Blake combined words and images to produce the celebrated illuminated books that are some of the most remarkable displays of visual form in Western aesthetics. Emily Dickinson used her manuscripts as canvases, her writing moving on them in ways that bear no resemblance to her poems as conventionally printed. In the twentieth century, James Joyce and William Burroughs each sought to expose the deep assembly codes—the hidden links and nodes—of the English language. Julio Cortezar wrote a novel entitled *Hopskotch* that asked its readers to choose their own pathways through its sequence of chapters. And Borges, in "The Garden of Forking Paths," "The Library of Babel," "The Aleph," and other stories anticipated hypertext as presciently as Vannevar Bush (and far more lyrically). All these writers and works have at one time or another been identified as "proto-hypertexts," meaning that they emulate in print many of the characteristic features of electronic hypertext despite the fact that they predate digital computers by decades or even centuries.

Given that, it is tempting to create analogies between, say, William Blake's illuminated printing—Blake's striking combinations of words and images—and modern hypermedia. Indeed, Blake has sometimes been called the first multimedia artist.

An illuminated print from Blake's *Songs of Innocence and of Experience*, copy Z. Courtesy of the *William Blake Archive*. Used with permission. http://www.iath.virginia.edu/blake/

Such analogies are valuable to the extent that they underscore the fact that electronic hypertext, far from being a radically new form of expression and communication, actually reflects some of the oldest language experiments on record. The nonlinear narrative mode traditionally ascribed to hypertext has a long—and frequently unacknowledged—ancestry in art and literature. At the same time, such analogies can become dangerous (or at least misleading) if taken too far: Blake, for example, was not, strictly speaking, a *multi*-media artist; in point of fact, he invented a new printing process (technically known as relief etching) that enabled him to combine words and images together on the *same* copper plate, the medium from which he then printed his books. This method was altogether different from that of the other printers of his day, who used letterpress typesetting in conjunction with engraving to print words and images via two technologically distinct processes. Examples like this remind us that analogies always have their limits, and that hypertext must finally be understood on its own terms, as a *computational* phenomenon.

Materiality Matters

Critical commentators on the medium have been fond of pointing out that unlike printed books, hypertexts are "immaterial": since they exist only as coded data in electronic space, hypertexts have no tangible forms the way a traditional book does. A hypertext is therefore not a "thing" or an object. Rather, a hypertext is simply patterns of light projected on a computer screen. For some critics this has been a point to celebrate, since it would seem to confirm the nonlinear freedom they believe to be inherent in hypertext. For other critics, these intimations of immateriality are an indication of an impoverished medium; they hold that even the most engaging of hypertexts lacks the sensuous look and feel of a leather-bound codex volume, or else they suggest that unlike printed books, hypertexts cannot be conveniently read in the bathtub (an apparently self-contradictory position, since owners of rare leather-bound volumes would be ill-advised to peruse them in bathtubs. . .).

In any case, although it is true that hypertext is insubstantial in a very narrow and literal sense—you cannot reach out and touch it—it is not necessarily helpful to think of hypertext as "immaterial." Various aspects of a computer's interface are very much analogous to the cover, binding, or typography of a printed book: as anyone who has ever used the same software package on both a Mac and PC knows, there are often minor (and not so minor) differences in its appearance, behavior, and performance. The computing platform therefore has a material impact on the presentation of electronic information. Moreover, hypertext—indeed, electronic data of any kind—is not really ethereal. It exists as an electromagnetically coded signal in a computer's storage system. What, then, are the implications of thinking about hypertext at a *material* level?

First, such thinking forces us to pay attention to the different platforms and systems that have historically evolved to support the conceptual ideal of "hypertext." Keep in mind that there is no one thing called hypertext—it is not an application or a program, not any one specific kind of product. Hypertext as a concept is not licensed or owned by anyone. As we have already seen by looking at one-to-many linking and guard fields, different hypertext systems, created and designed for different audiences at different times, have supported some very different features. These variations in the capabilities of one software or system as compared to another are unmistakably *material* differences in the technology—the fact that hypertext is not something you can physically hold in your hand is a red herring.

What practical difference does a software interface really make? Consider annotation. In electronic environments, annotation refers to the process of a user adding new text (or other kinds of content) to an existing document. Many early hypertext designers considered this to be a key feature of any viable hypertext system, not least because it greatly enhanced the interactive potential of the medium. Readers could do far more than simply personalize their hypertexts; they would become active participants in the text's ongoing re-creation and evolution, as other readers annotated the annotations, built new links between them, and so forth. Early hypertext enthusiasts saw this as one of the most distinctive and exciting examples of how hypertext would change the way we read *and* write.

Yet today, annotation is comparatively rare on the Web. It is true that some innovative sites do support it in one form or another, but this is by way of special enhancements like Java applets and server scripts. Annotation is not part of the standardized features of a Web browser. Yet one of the very earliest Web browsers, Mosaic (built, in part, by a computer science undergraduate student named Mark Andressen who soon after cofounded Netscape Communications Corporation) did support an experimental annotation feature that was later dropped by its commercial successor, Netscape Navigator. As this example illustrates, the way in which we use and understand hypertext is shaped not by the inherent limitations of the medium, but rather by software engineering and product design. Consequently, hypertext should always be thought of as part of the broader social contexts in which information technology operates. Marketing strategies, competition between rival companies, technical standards, usability testing, and intellectual property (in the form of copyright and patents) all have a direct and material impact on the way software works.

Changes in what "hypertext" is and has historically meant, from visionaries like Bush and Nelson, to the creation of early systems like Intermedia, Hypercard, and Storyspace, to the World Wide Web of today must be understood as part of a much larger process that depends upon the changing role of computing, communications, and information in society and culture.

Hypertext, HTML, and the Web

The World Wide Web is often described as a vast global hypertext, and indeed its content is presented on-line using a standard known as HTML (HyperText Markup Language). What sets the Web apart from any other hypertext system is that it is supported by the global networking protocols collectively called "the Internet" (which also support email, electronic file transfers, and other services). This means that users can access Web-based hypermedia from any computer with an Internet connection and the piece of software called a browser—as opposed to earlier hypertext systems, where the user needed to have the hypertext installed directly on his or her personal machine, or be logged into a mainframe computer. Moreover, the documents comprising a single Web-based hypertext may themselves be spread across computers located all over the world.

HTML is the lingua franca of the Web, and it is worth taking a moment to examine it more closely. HTML is not a programming language; it is a *markup* language (derived from a larger protocol called SGML, the Standard Generalized Markup Language). This means that HTML files are simply plain ASCII text files that include certain specialized "tags" (or markups); these tags convey information about how the text should be rendered and displayed by the Web browser. One can create HTML documents "by hand" simply by using a text editor (manually typing in the tags one needs) or by using increasingly sophisticated WYSIWYG ("What You See Is What You Get") software packages to produce complex graphical layouts. A very simple example of HTML code might look like this:

```
<b>The browser will display this sentence in boldface.</b>
```

The boldface "tag" is indicated by the angle brackets, which are opened at the start of the sentence and symmetrically closed at its end (the backslash character denotes a closing tag). HTML has evolved significantly since it was first tested in 1990, but even today it remains dependent on the same basic principles of textual markup.

We have already seen (from the example of a newspaper, above) that "text" encompasses a good deal more than just the linguistic "content" embodied by words and sentences. Text also has a pronounced visual and material dimension. This becomes particularly conspicuous in electronic settings where software like Photoshop and Quark can bend and morph letterforms into all kinds of unconventional shapes and arrangements. These fluid boundaries of identity between word and image are plainly evident in the graphic design conventions of the Web, where there has been an observable trend, directly proportional (or so it seems) to the commercial colonization of the Web, of forgoing unadorned ASCII text in favor of rendering site banners, buttons, logos, and the like as image files created with Photoshop or similar software. Likewise, a corresponding point could be made from the genealogy of the World-Wide Web Consortium's changing HTML standards, which have steadily provided the means for increasing the visual range of plain-vanilla ASCII text. Provisions for controlling font faces and point size, lineation, and the color of text are all now supported by various browsers. By contrast, HTML 1.0 (as the standard was called when it was originally drafted back in 1990) was very simple, consisting of only a dozen or so tags—no backgrounds, no tables or frames, no control over font color or face or point size—not even a <center> tag (!).

Tables are in fact another useful example here. Though it is true that they are used on the Web for the purpose for which they were intended—laying out information in orderly rows and columns—tables have also become the mainstay of graphic design on the Web, enabling authors to lay out Web pages in multiple columns and control the spatial arrangement of the elements on their pages. Even more recently, the advent of Dynamic HTML and Cascading Stylesheets (CSS) promises to continue increasing the range of visual control over text. Though its capacity for producing sophisticated typographic layouts is still quite primitive by graphic design standards (the equivalent of typesetting while wearing mittens), attention to HTML's continuing development reveals a pronounced bias toward the visual characteristics of even the most ordinary forms of text. This is one of the most distinctive aspects of hypertext on the Web, and the contrast to a system such as Storyspace—where control over the visual appearance of the text is quite limited—is noteworthy.

Because of its ostensibly "global" reach, the Web has often been celebrated as a radically democratic medium: a personal homepage is (theoretically) just as accessible as a mighty corporate portal. Perhaps there was once a time when this was true (though even the earliest search engines privileged the corporate hubs of the Web), but it is certainly not true today. (Also see "Political Economy," this volume.) Consider the following piece of unsolicited bulk email ("spam") that I received in response to one of the many Websites I maintain:[3]

> Dear Webmaster:
> Not all links are created equal. Some deliver surfers, some deliver browsers and most don't deliver at all.
>
> How would you like a link that gets a 75% clickthrough and all the visitors are shoppers already interested in what your selling?
>
> Only a link from the CatalogMart can deliver this qualified traffic.
>
> [. . . .]
>
> CatalogMart visitors are buyers, not "surfers"! Most of them come through the major online services and pay for their access. CatalogMart doesn't get traffic because it's pretty or fun. Our visitors come to the CatalogMart to request catalogs for products they are interested in buying by direct mail. They are not "clicks" or "hits" but real customers. And more than 75% of our visitors follow the links to our "Connected" sites.
>
> The cost of a link with descriptive text is only $100 dollars per month. An incredibly low price for directing thousands of interested shoppers to your site.
>
> [. . . .]
>
> Thank you for your time.
>
> Regards,
> [name and email address omitted]

This email message is an instance of what we might call "white-collar hypertext." It testifies to an emerging trend in which the plain and simple HTML link is taking on far more complex layers of social and commercial significance. If high-saturation graphic design was the first major stage in the corporate makeover of the Web, we are now witnessing the opening moves of a second, far more subtle stage, one in which the role of the HTML link, once the Web's great equalizer, is changing rapidly. In 1997, for example, Ticketmaster filed suit against Microsoft after Microsoft allegedly created an "unauthorized" link to Ticketmaster from a Web page located on a Microsoft server. To quote from the *Wall Street Journal*: "Ticketmaster maintains that the unauthorized link dilutes the value of its own sponsorship by companies such as MasterCard, and says that Microsoft was able to attract advertising to its Seattle Sidewalk site based on the Ticketmaster link. 'They want to suck up our content and keep the advertising revenue from it,' says Ticketmaster's CEO."[4] Several months later, the *Journal* reported that growing numbers of corporations were hiring attorneys to draw up "link licenses," legal documents which would govern the conditions of one site's linking to another: "'Links establish a connection between two businesses, and people really want to be able to control that,' says an intellectual property attorney."[5]

Web rings offer a further example of how the social and economic dynamics of the Web are refashioning hypertext in more restrictive modes. A Web ring consists of a series of sites devoted to a common topic with an agreed-upon linking protocol. Typically, wherever a user enters the ring, he or she is offered the option of proceeding forward to the next site in the ring or back to the previous one (or to a central administrative site, the hub of the ring). There are Web rings devoted to everything from Elvis to S/M. In 1997 *Investors Business Daily* reported that "The trend is rapidly gaining momentum—in January, Webring.com, a directory for Web rings, listed about 1,000 rings. By September, it listed 18,000, encompassing some 200,000 Websites. Webring.com estimates that its number of 'hits' is going up at a rate of 22% per quarter."[6] Another company, LOOPLINK, describes their service this way: "By sharing the site traffic among loop member sites, every LOOPLINK member benefits. Every time a new site is added to the loop, traffic within the loop increases, benefiting all loop members. It's like being in a popular mall. The loop is greater than the sum of its parts."[7]

Clearly the blatant consumerism of white-collar hypertext—its looplinks and Web rings and click-throughs and link licenses, the obsession with generating hits and traffic, the analogies to shopping and malls—points to hypertext having transcended the narrow concerns of computer science and cognitive philosophy, and emerged as a major commercial asset. All this seems a long way from the enthusiasm of the early hypertext visionaries. But even Ted Nelson was fond of pointing out that one of the attractions of his Xanadu system was that royalties could be paid directly to authors every time someone linked to one of their documents. So, for better or for worse, hypertext is part of the Web's emerging digital economy, and must be understood in this regard.

A Closing Word

Though it seems certain that what I have been calling white-collar hypertext will continue to dominate the commercial mainstream, it is also important to recognize that from its inception, hypertext has captured the attention of artists and writers. I have already mentioned Michael Joyce's pathbreaking electronic novel *afternoon*, which first appeared in 1987. Since then, a number of writers have experimented with hypertext fiction and poetry. A significant number of these authors have opted to create their work using Storyspace, one of the hypertext authoring systems that predates the Web and HTML. Their hypertexts are available on floppy disk from Eastgate Systems, whose URL is listed below—Eastgate's publications are indispensable to anyone with a serious interest in electronic writing. But growing numbers of writers have also turned to the Web, opting to reach their on-line readers directly. The Hyperizons site listed below offers one good index and starting point for hypertext fiction; likewise, the electronic journal *Postmodern Culture* regularly publishes innovative electronic writing (including a special issue devoted to hypertext in May 1997). Artists and writers will continue to help expand the horizons of hypertext development, much as they were some of the most aggressive adopters of the technology in the late 1980s and early 1990s. What will attract their attention? Kinetic or animated text (which Macromedia Flash is currently popularizing on the Web) and three-dimensional writing spaces (see my *Lucid Mapping*, below) are just two of the more obvious starting points for future invention and exploration. What is avant-garde today on-line often becomes mainstream tomorrow. Such is the inexorable dialectic of the Web.

Lucid Mapping: an experiment with three-dimensional hypertext. Courtesy of the author. http://www.iath.virginia.edu/~mgk3k/lucid/

NOTES

1. So wrote Vannevar Bush in his influential essay "As We May Think," originally published in a 1945 issue of *LIFE* magazine and reprinted in several places since—and also available on-line. Bush was not discussing hypertext per se, but rather hypothetical technologies for duplicating the brain's "associative" thinking.

2. See http://iberia.vassar.edu/~mijoyce/Ted_sed.html.

3. Email received Sunday, August 24, 1997 05:49:15 -0400 (EDT).

4. *Wall Street Journal*, April 29, 1997.

5. *Wall Street Journal*, July 2, 1997.

6. *Investor's Business Daily*, September 26, 1997.

7. Email received Tuesday, September 2, 1997 13:31:34-0400 (EDT).

Chapter 11

Narrative

Joseph Tabbi

Our tales are spun, but for the most part we don't spin
them; they spin us. Our human consciousness, and our
narrative selfhood, is their product, not their source.
—Daniel Dennett, *Consciousness Explained*

Participants in conversations on and about the World Wide Web have
made use of a number of terms to describe narrative qualities specific
to the on-line environment. Beginning with Ted Nelson's and Vannevar Bush's early attempts to organize and disseminate textual
materials through networked computers, a full-blown, specialized
vocabulary has been devised using such neologisms as "lexia,"
"docuverse," "structangles," and—the one word that may yet find
widespread acceptance—"hypertext." This unconventional terminology contributes to the much contested notion that linked computers
are a wholly new medium, supporting the theorist's claims to have
evolved a "fundamentally different way of thinking" within a "different paradigm" (Nelson 1995). The word "hypertext" itself, which
Nelson defined as nonsequential writing organized in blocks through
electronic links, is often meant to supplant some supposedly traditional (but, in reality, largely mythical) notion of narrative as a linear,
page by page movement from definite beginnings through intermedi-
ate complications to an ultimate resolution (in death, marriage, or—
more often in recent novels—social mobility). Supposedly, novelistic
endings are made palpable, and narrative closure is reinforced, by the
diminished number of bound pages as we finish reading a book, a
material satisfaction not available on the Web's open network.

In my own practice, particularly in editing and codesigning an e-journal for a general literary audience, I have shied away from the populist (but also specialized and needlessly bureaucratic) terminology of the literary technologists. Rather than reinvent a new vocabulary for acts of narration on the Web, I have preferred to locate those places where narrative theory and electronic parlance already converge. A rhetoric of "threads," "webs," "lines," "patterns," and "weaves" pervades day-to-day electronic communications, although the terms themselves are not left unchanged by their expansion into the domain of computer technology. My project then is in rough agreement with Jacques Derrida's efforts to generalize the term "writing" so as to cover the entire field of contemporary discourse. For what writing today is not "contemporary"? Now that the literary canon is being archived, tagged, cataloged, and cross-referenced, books will come down off the Harvard Classics "five-foot shelf" and be displayed instead in their cultural settings—the upper Manhattan of the Harlem Renaissance, or Shakespeare's Globe Theater, to name just two digital environments in existing virtual libraries.

"Making it new," the project of literary modernism, is today less a matter of renaming than of recycling and resituating the work and the words of past authors. So where neologisms miss the mark, we might instead practice what Derrida called "paleonymy, keeping the old name despite its radical displacement and the grafting of its usual connotations onto a new medium" (Krapp 1996:167). In this chapter, I will accordingly continue to speak of "narratives" rather than "hypertexts." (See "Hypertext," this volume.) But the word itself will need to be translated to a place—the objectless expanse of the Web—from which it is possible to look back on the technology of the book and to discover that narratives have always resisted linear form and struggled with the constraints of the print medium.

Given the material constraints on print narratives, we tend to forget that, at any point within the covers of a book, the inevitability of ending may be resisted or put off. Such resistance depends on syntactic, semantic, and symbolical structures much more than the particular lexical coding—that is, the arrangement of words or word groups that now can be identified and accessed electronically in any order, or in no order at all. It is telling, I think, that Nelson chose the word "lexia" to designate reading units in hypertext, since it is only at the lexical level that (barring puns and other accidents, oversights, or willful wordplay) readers can be fairly sure of a one-to-one correspondence between words and their cumulative meanings. If books could be neutralized in this way, they would easily be displaced by a nonsequential technology.

But that's not how books work—not when a passage can be *gone back to*, with a flip of pages that, while reading, is often easier than retracing the branching pathways through a hypertext. With the right kind of narrative repetitions and cognitive reinforcement, even the flipping of pages can be avoided. It would seem, then, that the celebrated nonlinearity of hypertext is in large part a literalization (at the level of tagged word groups) of mental connections that readers learn to make, one way or another, when reading print narratives. Through a kind of flickering or oscillating attention, such connections can easily take place across many pages. They enable a poem or a narrative to take shape in the mind of a reader, and this mental picture is rarely congruent with the progressive continuity of lines following lines and pages stacked on pages through the course of a book. Strictly speaking, it is only *after* the reader stops reading that the hypertext link becomes useful, not for establishing a narrative sequence but for producing and retrieving information, and finding pathways through lexia that have already been mapped out by the author during composition or the reader during previous readings.

Hence, one can claim a superior value for hypertext as a medium of associative *connection* only by ignoring the actual language in which any text is written (and the more literary the work, the more associative and nonlinear will be its text, generally speaking). Even the relative ease with which one can enter a hypertext at any point, in a structure whose visible outline has several immediate points of entry, has its analogues in print narrative. The start of a discourse in medias res, for example, is a device that never waited on hypertext—it was in fact originally an epic convention that got carried over from orality into print. Similarly, the conflation of beginnings and endings within a single print paragraph can make the newfound ability to start anywhere and then jump from one passage to another seem arbitrary by comparison. It is easy to cite examples in printed texts when one thinks one has reached an end—say, after a treacherous stretch of driving in bad weather—only to find that one is in fact just beginning:

> The rain had stopped. I could forget about the curved warning signs; the gently winding road, which conformed so gratifyingly to my map, would dry fast. I settled back in the driver's seat and accelerated. The steering wheel came off in my hand.

In this fine opening paragraph of Harry Mathews's print novel, *The Journalist* (1997), a driver traveling along a well-mapped road is surprised out of himself. No longer able to distinguish between what is inside and outside, his sense of personal identity is revealed to have been, at every moment and without his knowing it, a cognitive fiction:

> The possibility had always been real. You never had to remind yourself of it. And it remains real. At such a moment, who are you? Where are you? You cannot dismiss the question by observing that "you" have become a mere object manipulated by the indifferent laws of physics. One part of you says that; another part listens. What and where are they? What and where is your identity? (*The Journalist* 3)

A part of us speaks and another part listens, as if our very sense of a stable and continuous self were nothing but a *narrative* that we tell ourselves, a "world fiction" that under normal circumstances seems continuous and linear. However, at any moment, given a sudden change in our environment, our sense of self can be revealed to be fundamentally fragmented and permeable—a webwork of signs and divergent discourses vying for attention (and continuing to jostle with one another in our minds, after they have receded from consciousness).

That is how narrative is imagined by the graphic artist Anne Burdick, in a series of images—also based on travel by car—introducing a collection of critical hypertexts entitled "image + narrative." Broken white lines move beneath the car's wheels like a needle through a textile; a suburban street seen through a rearview mirror settles on a homemade road sign, reading: "You've got our attention." The journey remains the mythic reference for all narrative, except that now the illusion of continuity is broken up, for Burdick as for Mathews, by the medium of representation. Through a frame that recalls a TV screen, we see the lines and the reflected images as discreet elements in a digital field—aspects of the woven "thREADs," or inscribed reading pathways, that define Burdick's site design.

On first looking into "image + narrative," readers are presented with a series of animated graphic image files. Through a frame that recalls a TV screen, scenes from a road trip—a staple of narrative continuity—appear as discreet elements in a digital field. White lines passing underneath a car and a variety of signals in a rearview mirror, all vie for attention in a field of competing discourses.

With this visual example, we can perhaps begin to specify what it is that changes, fundamentally, when we move from print to hypertext reading. In hypertext we are given a multiplicity of sources and texts for browsing, so that image and narrative, the verbal and the visual, all exist on the same plane. Even the near and the far, as hypertext poet Stephanie Strickland (1997) has written, are "equally present, and equally speedily present." Where a book can only *refer* to the texts and images it cites, a Web page can, in theory, actually present its electronic citations directly, through the clickable link that brings the environment into the screen space. The outside is thus ready at any moment to become the inside. This permeability—more than the actuality of any particular link or set of links—is definitive of reading in electronic environments.

To the extent that we have hypertext only through a series of mediations—our screen that brings the environment *in*, our browsing software, the electronic desktop that lets us customize image and text for further processing, and the like—we need to be that much more aware of our collaborative activity while reading. Because the animated graphic image file puts us in the position of the driver, an observer of the changing scene behind and in front of the car, we're doubly mediated. Looking through both the windshield or mirror and the enframing TV screen, we find ourselves in the position of an *observer observing herself*. This second-order observation is at the heart of any narrative transit through electronic landscapes. In fact, I would again insist that the celebrated "nonlinearity" of hypertext reading and its purported mindlike character, have more to do with the renewed centrality of such reflexive, second-order positioning within the electronic environment than with the specific means—the browser and its clickable link—of moving around in that environment.

That we know the world only through particular frameworks, categorizations, and preestablished expectations is brought home to readers by the very look of *The Journalist*, in which paragraphs are numbered, and then renumbered and subdivided in an elaborate and doomed attempt to match the language to the atomistic world of facts and perceptions. The project is doomed because, unlike the semiotic model of a network of signifiers linked with each other and their signifieds, the identity of the world is a composite of attributes that only come into existence as they are observed. Even the shoes that the journalist's colleagues wear to work or the sunlight falling across a secretary's telephone become distinct (and thus capable of relating to one another) only as they are newly noted in the journal; only then do they "emerge from the strangeness of systems outside" the journalist's control, as the clarity of his own evolving system plunges endlessly into the obscurity of these "systems outside" (*The Journalist* 9). As noted attributes take form in clusters shaped in a network of coded relations, Mathews's novel circles away from any notion of journal writing as the objective reporting of some preexisting world out there; only in the notation are objects and events "naturalized" (*The Journalist* 9). At the same time, the novel also avoids attributing purposeful creation to the writer-observer. Instead, as the novel's narrator discovers to his surprise, the journal has a life of its own, its purpose a mere reflection of the categories with which the category maker approaches the world.

Mathews's "journalist," a man who has recently suffered a nervous breakdown, has been advised by his doctor to jot down "everything" that happens to him (*The Journalist* 8), "from how much he has spent on books and movies to what he eats" (dust jacket). But "everything," he soon discovers, is already caught up in its own networks of relations, and each item can belong to more than one category and can objective; B = what is subjective. The previous secondary divisions represented the same subcategory in both A and B: 1 = what involves others; 2 = what concerns only myself. These numbers have been replaced by the Roman numerals I and II and subdivided thus:

A
  I
    a = communication of some kind
    b = other actions and events
  II
    a = cultural events (all entertainments)
    b = other matters

B
  I
    a = things observed
    b = other people
      (ideas, feelings about)
  II
    a = dreams
    b = "thoughts about"
      (e.g., planning future)

B II/b   While these subdivisions increase thoroughness and accuracy, they should themselves be broken down more precisely. (For example, A II/a should be separated into "reading" and "other.") When I've finished cataloging the day's incerpts, I shall move to this next level of classification.

There's no denying that rearranging the incerpts is laborious, and each ramification will make it worse. Would indexing be more efficient? I must look into the possibility.

A I/a   When Gert came in to say good night, he was holding a book, his index finger marking a page. It was

Plutarch's life of Pericles. A sentence had been underlined and my name penciled in the margin. It read: "These things coming into my memory as I am writing this, it would be unnatural for me to omit them." Gert said, "It reminded me of your project." I was touched by Plutarch's words, if not in a way that Gert could guess. My Memorials had, as it were, been authorized, and literature had provided me with a distinguished colleague. Like Clara Schumann's music, the coincidence of Plutarch's opinion with my own confirmed me as a journalist – not yet a master, but no longer the beginner I so recently was.

TUESDAY, 6:30 A.M.

A II/b   With notes on this morning's dream in hand, I first must write down the improvements in classification that I imagined last night. While getting ready for bed, I mentally extended the example of dividing A II/a into "reading" and "other." The results are provisional, but I shall nevertheless start using them today.

A
  I
    a
      .1 phone calls
      .2 letters
      .3 conversations in person
    b
      .1 culture and entertainment
      .2 other
  II
    a
      .1 reading
      .2 other
    b
      .1 money matters
      .2 health
      .3 mundanities (e.g., what I eat)

The protagonist of Harry Mathews's novel, *The Journalist*, produces a print hypertext when he tries to note down "everything" that happens to him, as it happens. Like print, e-text is a framing medium within which readers and writers become category makers, builders of systems, and self-conscious observers of their own observations.

operate at several different levels. Initially he tries to distinguish "between fact and speculation, between what is external and verifiable and what is subjective," but this does not prevent the one from mingling into the other (*The Journalist* 20). Increasingly he finds his own consciousness getting in the way of such distinctions, to the point that his work on the journal itself—as his obsession with it grows— inevitably overwhelms his nonwriting "life." Reaching a trigger point in the narrative, when the writing of the life overtakes its living, the journalist abruptly realizes that his "laborious classifications have proved worthless" because in filtering the world onto the page, he has "left out the chief activity of my life and the chief fact of my project: the keeping of this journal. . . . The making of each page, the making itself, deserves to be accorded its supreme place" (*The Journalist* 190–191).

This paradox of self-inclusion—which Paul Harris (1999) in an essay on Mathews identifies as the "Tristram Shandy paradox"—could well be the source of nonlinearity in narrative fiction, whether in print or on-line. From Lawrence Stern (author of *Tristram Shandy* in the eighteenth century) to postmodern metafictionists such as John Barth, Raymond Federman, and Thomas Pynchon, and on to hypertext novelists Michael Joyce, Stuart Moulthrop, Mark Amerika, and Shelly Jackson, there has always been a powerful strain of self-reflexive writing that has challenged more conventional, "realistic" narratives. Self-reflexivity is certainly central to any conception of narrative on the Internet, which is as yet (and will be for some time to come) a space where *writing* is produced and exchanged at every moment throughout the "real world." This includes, as Robert Coover (1992) notes, "the world of video transmissions, cellular phones, fax machines, computer networks, and in particular . . . the humming digitized precincts of avant-garde computer hackers, cyberpunks, and hyperspace freaks" (1992:11).

The Web is, in short, a collective realization of the journalistic desire to note down—literally—"everything," even as this totality changes out from under us, moment by moment, with every new post. It is increasingly the case that hypertext fictions read like journal entries on a Beat road trip (examples include Rob Wittig's *Rude Trip* or Scott Rettberg, William Gillespie, and Dirk Stratton's *The Unknown*). Self-display is also a natural mode for the wired environment, and homepages have a tendency to be literal minded—as in the bedroom of the teenage girl that can be viewed by videotape twenty-four hours a day on the Web, or the continuous postings by thousands of listserv logomaniacs who reproduce the conundrum—without the self-consciousness experienced by Mathews's journalist, when the writing of the life becomes its living. The Web will always be ahead of our representations. And so, to go on living *and* writing, to avoid falling into paradox, writers on the Web need to learn to hold lightly to their own representations, and to be ready continually to reenter the on-line narrative stream that forever outruns consciousness.

The post–print medium's difference lies not in its linearity or nonlinearity as such, but in this potentially infinite connectivity in which all writing exists simultaneously with all other writing, so that one can no longer pretend to an objective position "outside" the written environment where life is increasingly lived. In such a circumstance, when collaboration is a condition of reading and narrative progress is realized in a branching series of clickable links, the creation of a sequence (by an author) ceases to be consequential for a reader. The condition of reading—if one is really on the Web and not attending single-mindedly to a self-contained site—is open to interruptions from any number of on-line discourses, both visual and verbal, competing for the reader's attention.

In itself, of course, interruption is nothing new: since Coleridge if not before, the man from Porlock seems to be always at the door, trying to sell you something just when inspiration is about to kick in. On the Web, however, the constant interruptions and cries for attention never interfere with the human browser's fundamental solitude. Suspense is dissipated because, in following a repertoire of programmed choices, no sustained engagement is possible with a single author or imaginary Other who will guide you through the fiction—as the Victorian patriarch guided his "Dear Reader," or as Virgil offers guidance that Dante is loathe to give up midway through their journey. On the Web, there is no getting around the fact that, in the task of writing one is, as one always has been, "totally alone, and it cannot be otherwise" (*The Journalist* 67).

In such solitary (and occasionally solipsistic) circumstances, is narrative even possible? I think so, but here is the point where we may have to inflect the word's meaning slightly away from its popular sense. "Narrative," if it is to again realize its all-important *cognitive* function in the new writing spaces, may well need to disassociate itself not only from its guiding source in a single authorial imagination, but also from the concept of *story*. Already one critic of hypertext, Linda Brigham, has suggested that objections to current hypertext fiction may be, at bottom, not that it is not any good, but that it is *not fiction*. That is probably true of the diaristic, self-involved, and largely performative writing that one tends to find on the Web. It is certainly true of the unprecedented flowering of a golden age of electronic correspondence, which (as Wittig has remarked) ought to lead to a resurgence of the eighteenth-century epistolary novel.

There is already a powerful, if somewhat neglected strain in American journal-writing—Paul Auster in *The Invention of Solitude*, David

Markson in his two most recent books, Lynne Tillman in her novels and art journalism, Mathews himself, and the novelistic journalism and journalistic fiction of William T. Vollmann—that has something to say to a popular audience newly migrating to electronic environments. Because this audience is already made up of aspiring writers, correspondents, and video and graphic artists, its members might even be more receptive to forms of narrative experimentation than a generation of readers nurtured by commercial film and TV. To the corporately controlled media can be left the telling of stories. We should look to the Web for something else: the emergence of narrative selves.

Chapter 12

Authorship

Russell A. Potter

It is obviously insufficient to repeat empty slogans: the author has disappeared; God and man died a common death. Rather, we should reexamine the empty space left by the author's disappearance; we should attentively observe, along its gaps and fault lines, its new demarcations, and the reapportionment of this void; we should await the fluid functions released by this disappearance.

—Michel Foucault, "What Is an Author?"

1st peasant: I'm not dead.
Cart driver: 'Ere, he says he's not dead
2nd peasant: Yes, he is!
1st peasant: I'm not dead. . . . I'm getting better!
2nd peasant: You're not. You'll be stone dead in a few
  minutes!

—*Monty Python and the Holy Grail*

The "death of the author" has been a central trope and tenet of recent criticism for decades; indeed it has become something of a first principle of literary theory in general. Yet in some ways, the author was already long dead; at least since the ascendance of the "New Critics" in the 1950s, the "authorial fallacy" served as the first official notice of this event, if not as a particularly profound assessment of what such a death might mean in a broader philosophical sense. Despite all these multiple notices and certificates of death, however, the "Author" has continued a lively postmortem existence, at least as a kind of named, translucent overlay, in many works of contemporary literary history and criticism. This is due, in part, to fields of criticism, such as Marxist and feminist theory, within which the identity of the author—even if in a sense only a symptom of subjective categories such as gender and class—has remained central to the act of reading. And yet there is something more to this endlessly deferred demise than the utility of something called an "Author" to a particular narrative of subjectivity or political position, some strange way in which we, as Foucault himself admitted, have allowed the names of authors to function "ambiguously," naming at various times a discourse, a "body of work," a style, a school, or a persona. Foucault himself—like Barthes, Kristeva, and the rest—has *as a name* underwritten an entire galaxy of discourses ostensibly derived from his work, somehow "of" him, somehow "Foucaultian." As the name of the Critic supplants that of the Author, the weary student may be forgiven for thinking that this brave new critical world bears an uncanny resemblance to the old world of "Authors" and their affects that those critics worked so diligently to defuse.

One of the reasons that this is so, curiously enough, is that the very media which were supposed to disperse and alienate the affective "aura" of the author have instead resuscitated the power of authorial presence. We are never so easily persuaded of authors' dramatis personae as when we see them interviewed on television, banter with them in an on-line chat, or listen while driving to their voice reading from a cassette tape. The speed and multiplicity of modern media have swept the Author, along with other hitherto reclusive souls, into the spotlight; without the book tour, the spot on *Good Morning America*, and the dustjacket photo, there would apparently be no audience, or at least such are the dictates of the publishing world. Now we buy our books at Barnes & Noble, and cart them home in shopping bags etched with the faces of Charles Dickens or Virginia Woolf, or—better yet—we read them online, browsing the labyrinthine corridors of the World Wide Web, grabbing a free novel or a poem from a text-based public archive, or ordering a paperback from Amazon.com. As a label, at least, the Author is vital to all these processes; far from receding into anonymity, the Author today is more visible than ever—at least if we mean the canonical, well-known "Author" who comes equipped with criticism, MLA sessions, and scholarly Websites. This lively canonical Author, however, is surrounded like Odysseus at the borders of Hades by a thousand anonymous and thirsty souls, whose names and faces are lost in the blur and buzz of discourse, whose texts, though they circulate in the same on-line "space," are rarely marked with a name, and possess an anonymity to rival the most fragmentary and enigmatic medieval manuscript.

For the mass of our discourse comes unnamed. This has been true at least since the ascendance of the magazine in the mid-nineteenth century. In this day when printed magazine articles almost always carry a byline, it is hard to recall that whole periodicals, such as Charles Dickens's *Household Words* or *Punch*, ran for years with nary a byline for anything but longer, serialized pieces. The periodical "works," indeed, of a Dickens or a Poe or a Thackeray, who had their hands in dozens of magazines, are always diffused, and many may never be proved on or against them due to lack of evidence. Beyond them, amidst them, a crowd of literary day laborers churned out topical essays and book notices week after week, their only satisfaction that of seeing their texts in print, and receiving a modest payment to aid them in stitching a sustenance together. Some, like Henry Morley, who wrote for Dickens's periodicals, were astonishingly prolific, penning hundreds of unaccredited essays on every topic under the sun; others surfaced only for one enigmatic submission. The "magazine" took its name and its textual ethos from its metaphorical ancestors; it was a storage cabinet of curiosities, a reservoir for textual ammunition, a warehouse of vendible goods. And, far from seeing its dispersed and vast textual surfaces as a dilution of the intensity of discourse, there were many who, like Edgar Allan Poe, saw the rise of the magazine as the quintessential medium of an era, a bold new possibility whose new discursive patterns were a spur to creativity, the herald of a new age of letters.[1]

The World Wide Web, not yet a decade old, bears a curious resemblance to its nineteenth-century forebears. If the magazine was a hierarchical storage cabinet, with its features, its minor articles, its letters, and advertisements, the Web was a horizontal, rhizomatic structure, with endless potential cross-connections but no clear center or summit. Magazines which tried to move themselves onto the Web without translating their paradigms often failed to find an audience for this very reason, since structural elements such as "covers," "tables of contents," and "features" were often blurred by readers who entered laterally, browsed a few random bits, and departed without ever arriving at the ostensible center or beginning of an "issue." In contrast, magazines and 'zines succeeded because they had dynamic content lists rather than segregated "issues," onboard search engines, and a floating masthead which followed the reader from page to page (often silently tracking the habits of readers by exchanging "cookies" with their browsers). The readers interpellated by this new medium tended to be affluent, restless, and fickle—leaping from an article in the *New York Times* on-line to a collectible toy site, an on-line auction house, and their second cousin's homepage. Cast into this new medium, authors found themselves in a similarly nomadic space, where freelancers outnumbered paid writers by a hundred to one, and a very low value was set upon writing produced in or for the on-line environment. For some, such as the writers of 'zines and fan pages, this was no deterrent, as the pleasure of placing their texts on-line was its own reward. But for writers who traditionally had eked out some kind of a living in print, the Web offered only the vertiginous thrill of seeing one's text slip out of one's own hands, endlessly copied and retransmitted.

A similar vertigo accompanied the height of the magazine era in the mid-nineteenth century. There was no international copyright, and very little in the way of effective enforcement of U.S. copyrights; it was this situation that drove Poe to declare that "American writers may as well slash their throats."[2] American magazines routinely filled their pages with features taken from British periodicals, and reprinted pieces from their own and other periodicals' past issues, usually without the author's permission or any additional compensation. Capable writers, such as Poe himself, had to try to place their best work more than once; as an editor, Poe was one of the most efficient self-plagiarizers ever, to the extent that many of his tales and essays saw print a half-dozen times in as many years. There was an apparently endless appetite on the part of readers, who gobbled up texts by the bushel, hungry for quantity and variety; loyalty to any one periodical was thin, and many journals, even the successful ones, had to frequently shift their styles and strategies to retain readers, or find new ones. Not surprisingly, many periodicals appeared, flourished, and collapsed within a year or less—with their editors and writers quickly seeking, and finding, places elsewhere on their demise. Rarely had there been so many pens so busily employed, yet with so little security and recompense.

The Web, already infamous for the fickleness of its vast audiences, has given many on-line authors similar treatment. Yet unlike the magazine, where the physical costs of production and materials often doomed an operation, the Web is apparently free of such constraints; the producer of an on-line 'zine has only to pay the monthly rent for a modest amount of server space—perhaps $25 or less—and invest his or her own time and energy. Yet oddly, commercial e-zines have become notorious money losers, as conventional publishers still seem to believe that a magazine requires a large paid staff whose salaries will at some point be covered by advertising revenue. True, the more elaborate kinds of content—frames, tables, in-line video and graphics— can be time-consuming to produce, and running a server capable of handling hundreds of simultaneous calls for data can be costly as well. Yet even academic journals, whose production needs are relatively modest, have not always found that on-line publication reduces their costs; the dream of the Internet as a realm of "free" discourse has eluded academia—ironically one of the first homes of the Internet in its precommercial days.

It's odd to recall that, scarcely a decade ago, the Internet was primarily a conduit for academic and government communication. Initiated by a consortium of researchers and officials at the U.S. Department of Defense, most of the Internet's original "nodes" were located on servers at the larger research universities. The first users of this resource were bureaucrats and technocrats, but academics in other fields soon found access to its resources invaluable for their work. This old "noncommercial" net was not in fact *free*—it relied quite heavily on government subsidy and the financial support of host institutions—but it had the appearance of being so. Faculty and graduate students from places as far-flung as Omaha and Tel Aviv could now send each other calls for papers, bibliographies, and drafts of research papers at no perceptible cost, and with a speed far greater than any comparable means of communication. Eventually, automated email lists created the possibility of an on-line "discussion," where responses and rejoinders were copied to every participant, thereby enabling the production of "threads" of discourse that crossed all kinds of national and regional boundaries. The earliest academic electronic journals, such as *Postmodern Culture*, grew up in this space; the masthead and table of contents were echoed to an email list of subscribers, who could then either request the issue from a list's server or log on via an anonymous ftp (file transfer protocol) to download the various pieces of each "issue."

When the Internet was opened to commercial traffic early in the 1990s, the cat was let out of the bag. More accurately, any number of cats were let out of any number of bags, since anything that could be copied likely would be. Even then, the commercial viability of the Net would have been minimal had it not been for the emergence of the World Wide Web, initially a European system for exchanging scientific research. Because the Web supported visual as well as textual materials, and because it assembled these into recognizable "pages" of information, the old system of servers, gophers, and ftp sites became instantly obsolete; the search, retrieval, and assembly of on-line information was achieved simultaneously and invisibly. Yet at the same time, a new layer of labor was introduced into the hitherto low-gloss surface of electronic space; the days of e-zines, during which typographical errors, blips of ASCII art, and widely varying styles of presentation were part of the appeal, were suddenly numbered. Suddenly, readers were also "consumers," and their daily bread of information now came wrapped in a colorful cellophane bag of banner advertisements, cross-links, and free limited-time offers. In order to produce the glossier and more labor-intensive content, many Web authors—now known as "content producers"—opted to accept advertisements and cross-links to defray the cost and labor of meeting these new expectations. With each side of the equation feeding the other, there was a new kind of vertigo, in which yesterday's exciting Website packed with graphics was today's dull and lifeless relic—where were the streaming videos, the background, the sound samples?

The impact of this change registered, ultimately, even in the very places where the noncommercial, "free" text model was first proclaimed—at *Postmodern Culture*. *PMC* had originally asked its contributors to sign a contract that would permit any kind of noncommercial use or storage of the text, with permission needed only for use which constituted republication. Even then, only the author's permission was needed; the journal merely expected to be notified, since the copyright notices were made in the author's name:

> Copyright © [name of author], 199x, all rights reserved. This text may be freely shared among individuals, but it may not be republished in any medium without express written consent from the author and advance notification of the editors.

Since these texts were about as unglamorous as possible—using only ASCII characters and carat signs for footnotes—it was perhaps assumed that they were unlikely to be "published" again except on paper. A number of essays from *PMC* were in fact published in book form by Oxford University Press, then the journal's publisher, but this differed little from what had for years been the practice, say, between *Yale French Studies* and Yale University Press.

Oxford, despite its admiration for *PMC*'s project, was beginning to ask some of the same questions it asked of other academic journals: "Will we be expecting any revenue from advertising?" and "How do we sell a subscription to something that is given away, free, to anyone with Internet access?" Subscribing libraries originally received *PMC* on a computer diskette, a seemingly "hard" medium compared to an Internet archive, but it quickly became apparent that such a medium was inferior to the on-line archive—it could only be used on one type of computer, and was liable to loss, damage, and obsolescence, whereas the on-line text was continually available and relatively independent of operating systems and machines. The move to hypertext, in turn, made each issue more labor-intensive and increased the pressure to somehow make *PMC* a pay-per-view journal on par with other restricted on-line databases. In resisting this model, the editors of *PMC* came up with a mode of selling access that was truly unique: new issues would be available for free, but previous issues (the "archive") would only be available to subscribers, along with an efficient on-line search engine. It was under this model that the publication of *PMC* moved to Johns Hopkins University Press, where it became a part of Project Muse, a collection of searchable on-line journals. Only *PMC* and its younger cousin *theory & event* used this new model—and these were indeed the only journals on the list which had no paper equivalent.

The move to this new system, however, had some unforeseen consequences. Earlier contributors to *PMC*, who had signed agreements with the journal that used the relatively generous model of free use encoded by the original copyright notices, suddenly found that their texts could no longer be "freely shared." In fact, authors who taught at institutions who did not subscribe to *PMC* or Project Muse found that they could no longer access even their *own* essays. In response to the concerns of *PMC* contributors, founding editor John Unsworth set up an on-line email forum in which contributors and other concerned parties could discuss the issues raised with the editors and publisher. This forum, under the mock-scandalous sobriquet "l'affaire *PMC*," became both an exemplary and a notorious example of the conflicting interests of authors, editors, and publishers in the no longer free era of Internet publishing. *PMC* authors decried the "locking away" of texts that they actually wanted to distribute freely, or at least as freely as the Internet made possible. The editors countered that, unless a university press was going to get at least some revenue from subscriptions, they would be unwilling to bear the cost of production. The reverse-subscription model was debated at great length, with the authors at various points threatening to move off into an archive of their own, and the editors emphasizing the many hidden labor costs of the journal, and the need to somehow generate revenue. Paid advertising, paradoxically, was touted by the "contributor" side as an alternative to subscription revenue, but dismissed by the publisher as unlikely to produce enough money.

In the end, *PMC* did revisit its plan to have a pay-per-view archive; texts from the ASCII-only version of the journal were moved to a free archive directory, along with plain text versions of more recent issues. The full hypertext versions, meanwhile, remained accessible only to subscribers. It was a compromise, an improvement on the earlier system, but hardly an exemplary "postmodern" solution. With the authors clamoring for their rights and the editors and publishers talking "revenue," it could have been any conventional print magazine at stake, rather than *PMC*, the fairy godmother of the academic electronic revolution. *PMC*, it seemed, could not survive the transition from plain text to hypertext without capitalizing and territorializing its own pages to some extent. The cost of producing hypertext, however modest, was enough to start the serpent biting its tail; production costs necessitated recovery of costs, whether through subscriptions or advertising, and required that the whole text—or at least the best version of it—be locked away behind a barrier that checked incoming IP (Internet Protocol) addresses against a list of paid subscribers.

The implications of this practice of territorializing scholarly writing resonate startlingly with those for territorializing the "Author" with a capital "A." In the early days of the Internet, entities such as the "Project Gutenberg" led the charge toward providing free, on-line e-texts of canonical (and many noncanonical) authors. The pioneering texts were drawn from a variety of writings which had recently and not so recently entered into the public domain, mixed with texts that by definition were public: Edgar Rice Burroughs, Lewis Carroll, L. Frank Baum, the CIA World Factbook, and the free on-line ravings of T.A.Z. Most of these texts were simply scanned by using one or another type of OCR (Optical Character Recognition), and tended to have a fairly high number of typographical errors; there was no editorial apparatus, and the texts often contained cumbersome hard carriage returns that made them difficult to reformat. High quality, searchable archives of public domain texts seemed a next logical step—but as with *PMC*, a step that would likely be taken by those with a mind for "recovering costs." Scholarly reference publisher Chadwyck-Healey, whose reference CD-ROMs offered a thousand years of English poetry, was quick to move on-line, but only to subscribing institutions. The Oxford Text Archive offered some plain-text works on-line for free, but the more "edited" works had to be ordered with a credit card. The University of Virginia, parent of IATH, was another pioneer; it offered both public and proprietary archives, with those at UVA enjoying a fully searchable archive, and those outside able to search only "publicly accessible" texts.

Free archives were, in contrast, few and far between. Project Gutenberg grew, but not nearly as rapidly as first projected; anxieties over lingering copyrights and the tendency of the U.S. Congress to arbitrarily extend existing copyrights led to a long-winded legal caveat being attached to every Gutenberg text. The Library of Congress, with its American Memory Project, and the National Archives of Canada, both pioneered significant "national" on-line collections. Yet while the quality of content was high, the coverage was somewhat random, organized around a variety of loosely defined topics. With its all-collections search, however, the LOC's American Memory became the premier project of its kind, and as a public institution affiliated directly with the U.S. Copyright Office, it had a far wider rein in defining "public domain" and "fair use." As of 1999, dozens of collections—everything from early paper ephemera and documents in the Lincoln collection to films of the World's Columbian Exposition in 1901 and sound recordings of cowboys from the 1940s—could be searched for from a single central page. Copyright in most of these materials had either never been present (the materials being public records), expired, or had been assigned to companies or entities since defunct. What would the implication then be for materials in which issues of copyright still swirled around the authorial body?

Living authors, those who came to prominence in both the print and electronic eras, have shown a deep ambivalence, and sometimes outright hostility, to seeing their texts on-line. In a manner similar to the television writers who rushed to obtain and preserve some rights when their shows went into syndication, writers and their professional organizations hurried to lobby Congress for increased protection. Publishers, representing the vast body of works "for hire" whose ownership resided with them, lobbied even more fervently. The result has been that, with the exception of some up-and-coming writers desperate for exposure, very few writers have permitted their works to appear on-line. The Copyright Clearance Center, whose earlier mission was to license small runs of photocopied materials in the wake of the legal decision against Kinko's Copies, shifted easily to licensing on-line use—but only when the text in question was being used on a secure, password-protected site would permission generally be granted. The only notable exception to this widespread aversion to on-line publication of commercial fiction or nonfiction has been the practice, encouraged by the larger book reviews and newspapers, of licensing the first chapter of a work to appear on-line as a sort of teaser for the book as a whole; the *New York Times Book Review*, among others, routinely provides the first chapter of books it features, and many publishers do the same to encourage on-line browsers.

Yet while in terms of textual authorship there has been a reluctance to change, the music industry has provided a fascinating counterpoint, in that numerous artists have been extraordinarily eager to see at least some of their music on-line. The digital format known as MP3, which compresses a digitized song from 30–40 megabytes to 3–4 with little perceptible difference in sound quality, has been the gasoline of this conflagration, producing both odd bedfellows and unexpected animosities. In the early days of MP3, there were few enough on-line, and few enough people with the technology to download and decode them, that the music industry scarcely noticed (indeed, their complete lack of planning to either defend against or capitalize on this technology is perhaps the most mind-boggling error in recent memory for an industry with an old reputation for missing out on almost every trend). Yet as shareware and freeware MP3 players became more readily available, and with the introduction of inexpensive playback devices such as the RIO player to liberate these files from desktop computers, the revolution practically burned down the building before the major labels smelled any smoke. In 1999, the year of the digital music revolution, millions of MP3s were downloaded, but the music industry was still taking its time, planning for a unified format that could somehow protect the music from being copied without a fee being paid.

That same year, musicians who couldn't wait any longer took matters into their own hands. Chuck D, whose group Public Enemy had fought a bitter battle the previous year with its label DefJam when they tried to post the entirety of their new album on the Internet, moved to a new label Atomic Pop, which not only allowed but also encouraged the group to have a high on-line profile. The lead single from their new album was placed on-line as a free MP3, while the Atomic Pop Website took advance orders for the full album—which would ship to on-line buyers weeks before it appeared in any store. A few weeks later, on-line buyers could download the whole album for $8 (as opposed to $10 for an on-line order or $14.99 in stores). Numerous other artists, emboldened by Public Enemy's move, set up their own on-line shops, or affiliated with on-line vendors. Not the entire digital revolution was free, of course—in many ways, the teaser tracks released as free MP3s were close cousins to the "first chapter" routine—but for artists whose work had long been out of print, as well as artists still seeking big label success, there was a motivation to give away much more. For these artists, many of whom had little or no revenue from major labels, giving away music was the perfect way to promote their concerts, prove they were commercially viable, and stir up careers that had long ebbed, or had yet to catch fire.

Largely on account of poor industry planning, independent companies led the way in all areas: free music (MP3.com), teasers and pay-per-listen (Liquid Audio, goodnoise.com), and on-line CD vendors (tunes.com, cdconnection.com). Truly free MP3s—with no security encryption or watermarking—remained a gray market; some artists deliberately released songs this way to "stir up buzz," but the bulk were still traded without royalties, technically illegal but almost impossible to police. Watermarked MP3s and self-expiring tracks formed a happy (or unhappy, depending on your view) medium. Liquid Audio, a small but persistent player, was the first to sell music in a format that included all possible options from free tracks, to expiring tracks, to encrypted and protected tracks. The Liquid Audio system, which relied on high-level encryption as well as a "passport" which attached the purchaser's address and credit card information to all downloaded tracks, was an effective cork in the piracy bottle — and yet its technology scared away some labels and many consumers, concerned about what such tracks might be good for if some other standardized format took over, and the software became obsolete. RealAudio, long a leader in low-fi compressed audio formats, jumped in with its own RealJukebox system, which switched easily between streaming lo-fi and downloadable hi-fi connections, and included the possibility of video. Many small labels, such as Rykodisc and Rounder, gravitated toward these technologies since so much of their business was with non-mainstream consumers who were used to not being able to find what they wanted to buy in stores.

Part of the difference with audio authorship, from the start, was its different juridical and ontological structure: a recording of music by more than one person already involved the question of multiple authorship, not to mention some division of spoils between the writer of a musical work and its performer, in cases where they were not the same. Composer's rights, underwritten by ASCAP, had long since been successfully challenged by performer's rights, as ensured by broadcast and performance-based groups such as BMI. Yet despite these organizations, musicians were significantly less likely to own their own compositions or performances than those who plied their trade in print: sidemen and backup singers were easily labeled "workers for hire"; new acts were coerced into signing deals in which the label retained all performance and publication rights; older performers and composers had often lost their rights in label shuffles and publishing mergers. Such an unevenly enfranchised group was certainly more prone to take an interest in ways around the recording companies' usual methods of collecting (and often alienating) the fruits of their labor. Moreover, unlike the consumers of texts, music listeners tend to be both more nomadic and more obsessive, choosing new music unpredictably, yet seeking out particular older music with manic tenacity.

Authorship, in its juridical sense, is eminently alienable. The curious spectacle of Paul McCartney vying to buy back the rights of his own Beatles compositions from Michael Jackson is but one larger dramatization of a widespread artistic struggle. You can sell the rights to what you create and, as Superman® creators Seigel and Shuster discovered, spend a lifetime before you are able to recover even a tiny portion of what has been made on what you created. Print, in terms of novelists and best-selling nonfiction writers, has been kinder to its authors, with many able to retain copyright—but in the world of commercial newspapers, magazines, and screenwriting, the author is as liable as her or his musical cousin to see such work spirited away as "for hire." The Web has, if anything, vastly increased the stakes in this struggle; it is a technology readily capable of putting texts back in the hands of their authors, and yet it can with equal ease lock anything up behind firewalls, password systems, and encryption paradigms. Yet curiously, it is the "publisher" of texts—as well as musical or visual works—whose stake may well be the shakiest; since placing materials on the Web is tantamount to instant "publication," a publisher no longer has any special power to make things public. If there is a text that some part of the public craves—be it the secret files of the KGB, the unreleased outtakes of the Fugs, or an endless loop of the Zapruder film—that public can beat as wide a path to the door of a single desktop computer as it can to some corporate Website filled with advertising banners and showy JavaScript. It can, in fact, beat a *wider* path.

So is the Author still absent? Can we gaze now more fully into the impact crater of her or his disappearance? Perhaps it would be more accurate to say that the Author has been *scattered* rather than obliterated, released into any number of unknown future assemblages and configurations, imprisoned, liberated, killed, resurrected, divided, and rejoined as bits of textual DNA in the countless petri dishes of the Web. Do we want our Author with or without Bovine Growth Hormone? With or without textual apparatus or commentary? Will that be the trip-hop-glow-in-the-dark remix or the original twelve-inch vinyl from 1974? Yet in the Web's gardens of forking paths, oddly this seeming chaos can produce, when and where it is wanted, a perfect doppelgänger of the revered, edited, or illuminated texts of older days. Edited diplomatic editions of medieval manuscripts, the tear-stained pages of George Eliot's letters, the yellowing covers of periodicals printed during the Harlem Renaissance—all these and more have come, or could, to a computer terminal near us. Shrines to the Author, like Chaucer's *House of Fame*, grow ever more gothic and labyrinthine, with names fading and appearing in the blink of an eye, and our words, via electronic cables, really *are* carried up to heaven into these richly in-line-graphic-festooned halls. The old texts and paradigms are still with us, and can indeed move with us, as we move into new media, different computers and software, and different modes of reading, writing, or composing. At the feet of the colossal Ozymandius of our fallen Author, we seek ourselves in the Book of Sand, and as sands through this hourglass, so are, and will be, the (Internet-capable) days of our lives.

NOTES

1. "The whole tendency of the age is Magazine-ward," wrote Poe in 1845, adding that "in the end (not far distant), [it] will be the most influential of all the departments of Letters." Quoted in Kenneth Silverman, *Edgar A. Poe: Mournful and Never-Ending Remembrance*, p. 246.

2. Silverman, *Edgar A. Poe*, p. 247.

Chapter 13

Multimedia

Sean Cubitt

In the popular media, the great achievement of the
Web can be seen as the way it has drawn together
the sound film and television with the illustrated
magazine.

Defining Multimedia

The term "multimedia" has become one of the most overused and un-
derdefined words in our digital age. The basic premise is simple. All
digital media are at bottom simply patterns of zeros and ones of machine code that represent the flipping on and off of minuscule electronic
switches. This means that any input—texts, sounds, images, or numbers, whether you download them from the Web, type them in yourself,
or grab them from a CD-ROM or DVD—is transformed into binary
data. Likewise, the output from the computer—voice, image, sound, di-
agram, spreadsheet, and so on—is also an expression of the underlying
zeros and ones. You can easily imagine a program which will, say, meta-
morphose the text that you type in into music or change any algebraic
formulae into images. The widely used *Mathematica* software for high-
level mathematics does the latter as a matter of course, automating the
work of turning algorithms into graphs. At root "multimedia" means
that any data can be transformed into any kind of output. As a result,
the distinguishing features of writing, painting, or music making are
lost in digital media. As we will see, this has great importance for the
way digital communication design can be undertaken.

The word "multimedia" is often used in a restricted sense to refer specifically to CD-ROM and the newer types of storage media used to package encyclopedias, children's software, games, and other info-tainment products. Of course, the qualities of digital media are such that it is increasingly difficult to draw a line between what arrives in a stored form and what is accessed via the Web. A lot of materials that were formerly shipped to end users on CD-ROM can now be down-loaded, and many DVDs and CD-ROMs come with ready-made Web links to allow users to update information or play games on the Web. Nonetheless, since there is an industrial distinction to be made be-tween the Web and the multimedia industry proper, it is as well to keep the distinction in mind. In what follows, however, I will be using "multimedia" to refer to the convergence of previously distinct media in the form of Web publication and Web casting. The first thing we need to look at is the process of convergence that brings us to mul-timedia. Here we need to understand a little of the political economy of the electronic media, as well as something of the history of older media. (See "Political Economy," this volume.)

The process of convergence appears at first to be straightforward. What could be better than getting all your information and entertain-ment through a single, efficient, and relatively stable device like the Web? During the summer of 1999, search engines reported that the most popular search was no longer for "sex" but for "MP3," the new compression format for publishing music and other sound files on the Web. Does this statistic prove the popularity and success of the multimedia potential of the Web? Certainly it points us in that direc-tion. But as well as raising important matters of copyright, the MP3 format introduces another aspect of "multimedia": the economics of cross-media corporations. In the old days, print publishers, games makers, recording industry corporations, and film and television companies worked in their own specialist domains. Now, along with telecommunications companies, they must either work together or combine forces through takeovers and mergers to become even larger corporate entities capable, for example, of launching a product like *Star Wars Episode One: The Phantom Menace* (1999) simultaneously or in a planned wave of releases as film, toys, clothing, food packaging, games, videos, books, magazines, TV spin-offs, and Websites. This kind of launch, called "multimedia strategy," gains from the partici-patory culture of the Web: fans and critics alike will fill their own pages and the review areas of sites like Internet Movie Database with word-of-mouth that augments and expands the paid-for marketing of the cross-media product.

Thus, despite the apparent democracy of interactive criticism and participation, from the standpoint of corporate multimedia strategy the Web is merely one medium among others. No major film or album release is complete without an accompanying Website, and major corporations like CNN and the BBC have established Websites that at once promote and extend their offerings on their original media–cable and broadcast, respectively. In this way the boundaries between print publishing and Web publishing are becoming blurred. With the advent of digital television, there are many doubts as to the borders and relations between TV and the Internet. Some of these concern corporate ownership, and some of them raise important issues for design and implementation: the aesthetics of the Web. Though I will concentrate on the formal aesthetic challenges of multimedia, behind my observations lies a concern for the creative opportunities and challenges offered by the Web, and the way they appear to have been partially erased in the rush to turn the Web into another tool of mass marketing.

Mixed Media and the Problem of Control

The convergence of media appears to have been under way for at least a hundred and fifty years. Illustrated newspapers began to carve a major space in the popular market in the middle of the nineteenth century. Edison had encouraged experiments combining his two inventions, the phonograph and the moving picture, even before the first projected pictures in the 1890s. About thirty years later, the already monolithic film industry was finally forced to invest massive amounts of money in refitting all its cinemas for sound. In the same way, but starting from the opposite end, radio had a massively successful run of almost thirty years before it was transformed into television by the addition of pictures.

Throughout this history, there has been a kind of quiet panic about the virtues of the newer hybrid forms. Take the example of comic books. When the first comic strips began to appear in newspapers at the end of the nineteenth century, there was considerable unrest over the presumed damage they would cause to children's literacy (and later on, when horror comics became fashionable in the 1950s, there would be another panic over their moral effects). One of the recurrent criticisms has been that the more hybrid a medium becomes, the less difficult it is, and therefore the more it encourages a lazy cultural consumerism rather than an active cultural participation. The Web has attracted some of the same criticism. We use the word "browsing," for example, to describe that slightly bored, rather distracted way we have of flicking through illustrated magazines in waiting rooms or at the hairdresser's. Web browsing calls up the same cultural image of a type of reading that lacks engagement and focus, that is uncritical and lazy: the image it conjures up is of cows grazing placidly and contentedly without a thought behind their pretty brown eyes.

On the other hand, for two hundred years now Western aesthetics has been dominated by the idea that each medium has a special calling, and that great art follows that calling rather than the vocations of other media. Thus a true poet is one who engages with the meanings and sounds of words, the true novelist the one who addresses history and narration, the true painter the one who avoids both description and storytelling in order to concentrate on color and light. This pure "modernist" aesthetic came to a peak in the period in which abstract art, sound poetry, and serial music came to the forefront, among the avant-gardes of the early twentieth century. And today we find something similar. The most highly prized media, the media with the highest cultural value, are those which are the purest: music without MTV, books without pictures, and so on.

In the age of multimedia, however, we have begun to see a change in that aesthetic of medium-specificity. More recent music in the formal tradition, like that of John Cage or Iannis Xenakis, is accompanied by strongly visual scores and architectural light shows. Artists like Tom Phillips have challenged the "invisibility" of the book in works like *A Humument*, and contemporary art is so intensely conceptual that it makes no sense at all unless accompanied by words to enlighten us as to the idea behind it. Meanwhile in the popular media, the great achievement of the Web can be seen in the way it has drawn together the sound film and television with the illustrated magazine. Just as email has brought about a renaissance of the all-but-lost art of letter writing, so the Web has reintroduced text into the audiovisual world. And of course the computer itself has a growing cultural kudos: parents, for example, are happy to pay for a desktop machine and an Internet connection on the principle that anything to do with computers is educational for their children. The hybrid forms of multimedia have become key signifiers of the future-directed orientation of consumer computing generally and Internet services in particular in print and television advertising, often with vivid depictions of live-streaming video and video conferencing, services that are as yet beyond the reach of all but the most expensive corporate intranets. As a result, the older aesthetic of medium-specificity is left looking rather outmoded, while the up-to-date Web page is expected to display text and image at the very least, with probably an animated gif or two, and preferably downloadable audio or video files. Even static text can be reliably expected to come alive through Shockwave or Javascript effects.

With the possible exception of audio files, which still download at slower speeds than text and image, you would expect that this new hybrid form would provide designers with all the resources they could possibly desire. Of course, this is not entirely the case, and we arrive at the first crux in Web design: the degree of control the designer can have over the appearance of a page in an end user's browser. The most widely used standard program for Web design is hypertext mark up language or HTML. Using small fragments of coded instructions called tags, HTML instructs the receiving computer not only about the content of the page but also about how it should be displayed. Tags can specify the font the Web author prefers, background colors, and the order of images. But in terms of layout, HTML can only give the end user's computer instructions about the relative position of paragraphs, lists, tables, and pictures—relative, that is, to the edges of the window. Unlike word processing or desktop publishing packages, you cannot tell the end user what font to use, because he or she may not have that font installed. Since the whole purpose of HTML is to allow different kinds of computers to communicate in a common binary language, there is no guarantee that the page that displays will have as big (or as small) a screen as the designer's. Users may have set their other default settings to give them control over how your page is displayed. It is the user who has final control over the way an HTML page looks, not the designer.

More recent software applications allow the designer greater control over the final appearance of the page. Some derivations from

HTML like SGML, the parent program, and XML, the extended mark up language that combines HTML's simplicity with the wider programming possibilities of SGML, can specify, for example, the width of a layout. A number of plug-ins are available that allow desktop publishing pages and other design tool programmed files to be saved as HTML, in many cases also specifying the width of the image and the absolute placing of elements within it. And some Javascript applications require that the designer include information about placing "objects" (images or active areas) on the page. In addition, some tags (including the notorious <blink> tag), even HTML ones, let alone Java, are specific to one of the giants of the browser world, Netscape and Internet Explorer, effectively forcing a person to use that browser in order to see a certain effect or even to open the page at all. Not only is this against the very principle of open and shared code on which the Web is based, but it presents designers with an aesthetic and moral dilemma.

How much control should a designer take? In the old days of medium-specific culture, the answer was clear. The artist was the sole author, and accepted the responsibilities as well as the rights that went along with the possession of rare skills and the opportunity to communicate through them with the nonartist public. But the Web has been conceived as a space in which the end user is in control, rather than the artist or the broadcaster. Even if the user makes scrambled eggs out of your carefully designed page, that is after all his or her choice. If users want to view without frames, without advertising, or even without images, that is their prerogative. So goes one side of the argument. On the other hand, as the Web becomes a more commercial and a more populous culture, with many users far less computer literate than the early pioneers, many designers want their pages to shine, and to do that, they need more control over the way pages will appear in the browser. And since monitor screens are standardizing, isn't it legitimate to expect that the vast majority of users will have their screens set to accommodate the widest image, and design to that specification?

These choices represent a real crux for multimedia applications: should the bias be toward the designer or the user? One way of making the choice is to decide whether your page is going to be most valuable because of its visual appearance or because of its content. Since the majority of content is still (though by no means exclusively) textual, the site that has a lot of data to communicate, like academic, scientific, and professional sites, will opt for a bias toward end users and the variety of machines, browsers, and defaults they are likely to use. If the site is more visually oriented and has less textual content, the designer may be tempted to take more control over the final appearance of the page. But these choices are governed by more ideological concerns. Multimedia applications allow the designer to decide not only what the page should look like, but how the ideal user should look at it: which browser, what screen ratio, what monitor settings, what depth of color, which font set, and so on. The problem lies in the idea of an ideal consumer for multimedia Websites. The common wisdom is that end users always have the final say, on the Web or watching television—they can surf another channel, or switch off, and, in cultural studies terms, they always have the power to interpret what arrives on the screen. But there is an equally common belief that the media we consume do make a difference: this is why advertisers and politicians spend so much money on the Web, and why artists believe it is worth intervening in computer networks as well as galleries. To better understand these issues, we need to look at some of the possible ways in which the convergent media can interact in multimedia environments.

Historically, there have been three major ways in which the interaction between media have been described: hierarchical, organic, and dialectical. As we will see, there are also some new variations on old themes and some brand-new possibilities inaugurated by the Web. But an exploration of these three modes of multimedia practice will help us understand the options open to Web designers, and eventually to clarify the problem of the ideal user.

A Hierarchy of Media

In one of the most influential early essays on film theory, Erwin Panofsky, the distinguished art historian, claimed that the sound film was a clumsy hybrid of two incompatible art forms, the silent cinema and the theater. The reason for this failure, he argued, was that unlike earlier hybrid forms of art, the dialogue film had not sorted out a hierarchy of media. Theater, for example, had long subordinated the visual aspect of performance to the script. The equally ancient forms of song and dance had likewise long ago settled that music would be more important than words for singing, and movement more important than music for dancing. With the benefit of hindsight, we can perhaps look back and see where he went wrong: cinema, too, has its hierarchy, and I would argue that at the top of it sits the script, the studio's central device for controlling budgets, and the audience's major interest in narrative film.

Television offers a more interesting field of inquiry, however, since the order of hierarchies moves between sports, news, narrative, and highly visual segments like computer-generated logos. Some important television critics have argued that TV is also hierarchical, sound being its major organizing principle, perhaps because it still betrays its origins in radio, and is still "radio with pictures" when we dash in from the kitchen to see the goal we just heard acclaimed by the commentator.

Does the Web suggest a hierarchical organization of media? Sound clearly is a weak element in most Web pages, but in many it is their reason for existing at all. Sseyo's Koan plug-in for the Netscape browser, for example, uses cunning computer tricks to generate music using the end user's own local memory to work its way through a basically mathematical pattern of sounds which can run for some considerable time without repeating itself. *Project Gutenberg*, by way of contrast, is a major attempt to provide as much of the world's great literature as possible on-line, using volunteer labor to type or scan in and proofread thousands of pages of text. Nicholas Pioche's *WebMuseum* (http://www.oir.ucf.edu/wm/), on the other hand, is one of a number of sites devoted to displaying high-quality images of great works of art, a site in which text is at a minimum, and sound is relatively unimportant. Given this variety of sites, it is impossible to argue that the Web as a whole has a particular hierarchy of media, but it is true to say that individual pages do.

And where they have such hierarchies, how do they work? Let's take a familiar type of site, a fan page for some currently fashionable actor or actress, one where the author has collected a lot of jpegs and gifs of their favorite star. The central focus of the site is visual. But there will almost always be some text, often in the form of captions for the pictures. The caption here is dominated by the image, providing a little supplementary knowledge to help read it properly. Another site, for example one devoted to the study of philosophy, might spice up its drier passages with portraits of the great philosophers, or diagrams illustrating something about their theories. Here the images illustrate the text, and are subordinated to it, adding some supplementary data or some additional pleasures to lighten the load of serious text.

The alert reader may have already have noticed that I used the word "supplementary" twice in the last paragraph. This is a term with a powerful technical presence in contemporary thought where it is used to denote those marginal details which at first appear to have little significance, but which can reveal extraordinary things about the structure and meaning of the object in which they appear. In our examples, the captions to pictures of the latest pop sensation are at once an attempt to guide and control the reader's interpretation of the image and an admission that the image is open to interpretation. In the example of pop stars, and likewise with movie stars, the apparent gap between image and text can also be read as a structural absence of the page: the absence of the songs. This gap between caption and depiction is the place where there should be the missing element of movement.

In this sense, we could say that the hierarchy is fractured by the absence of its true dominant—music in the one case, moving images in the other. Or perhaps even more radically, we could argue that fan sites are always subordinating themselves to the absent presence of the stars themselves. Indeed, many argue that the glamour of stardom is an effect of the combined presence (on-screen or on stage) of a person whose true personality is always absent, in the sense that it cannot be grasped and shared by the fans. The fan site is simultaneously a claim to a special relation with the star and an admission that "I am not worthy," a submission to subordinate status which serves to magnify the star's aura.

What then of the dry philosophical site and its images of the old philosophers? Here the images serve to illustrate the text, and occupy the subordinate position. Philosophy is one of the disciplines that prides itself on a rigid observance of ordered rationality and the exclusion of emotional appeals, especially to the imagination. Much the same can be said of the human sciences and of science itself. The supplementary role of images, however, reveals a characteristic demonstrated by a number of recent critics: that philosophy shows a tendency to use a highly visual vocabulary—like the words "reveal," "demonstrate," and "show" in this sentence. Far from relegating the visual to the margins of philosophy, the use of illustration gives away its little secret: that it depends on the visual for its entire enterprise. Careful reading of scientific and sociological texts will show an equally strong tendency toward the imagery of images. Indeed, the philosopher Richard Rorty claims that if we recognize the visual basis of philosophical metaphors we will abandon the central claim that philosophy has always made; that it has a privileged access to truth. The little gap between text and image can become an abyss big enough to swallow philosophy whole.

Panofsky's call for hierarchies to order and control hybrid forms then appears to be misguided, since any hierarchy will run the risk of giving away its secrets, and even of destroying itself. Nonetheless, the principles of captioning and illustration are the commonest relation between text and image in Web design. This appears to be a hangover from print culture, in which publications are either image- or text-based, and reserve captions and illustrations for almost decorative purposes. This relation is particularly clear in pages devoted to news and current affairs, where text, even if kept to a minimum, tends to control the available reading of images. Changes in political temperature can alter the caption of one and the same picture, so that people who once were heroic freedom fighters have become insurgent terrorists. Moreover, since digital media are inherently manipulative, the photographs themselves, once guarantees of a certain, perhaps limited but nonetheless persuasive, authenticity of the events they depicted, have forfeited our trust. Ten minutes in an image-manipulation program and the weary, sparring opponents at a negotiating table have become fresh-faced, flushed with health, and considerably closer together.

But multimedia has brought with it another alteration in the text-image relation. One of my browsers has Palatino set as its default font; the other has Avant Garde. If I happen to look at the same page in both browsers successively, there are small differences in layout brought about by the different lettering. Like just about everybody else, I ignore them. To some extent, this is nothing new. Even literary studies tend to ignore things like typesetting, inks, and paper. But with the lack of control over end-user fonts, not only has the designer lost control over the layout, but to some extent the text has revealed that it too is manipulative. Few of us feel as certain of news read on the Web as we do of news published in more traditional media, even

TV. We are likely to try to confirm a news item that startles us on another site or in another medium. The manipulability of digital images has begun to infect the digital text as well. No wonder it is so hard to find a successful way of controlling Web design and content through hierarchies of media.

Organic Unity

Not only has multimedia become a complex and slightly suspect word; even the term "convergence" has begun to be challenged by a new coinage, the phrase "conversion media." The principle of this change is that not only have we gone beyond the multiple media toward a situation in which the different media converge with one another, but that a new phase is beginning in which the differences between media are only a matter of the conversion of data streams into one form of output or another. Aided by expectations of novel delivery systems for the Internet including low-orbit satellites, cellular technology, and fiber-optic cable, the Web seems closer than ever to providing live-streaming video and audio in real time. Under these circumstances, the differences between media become a matter for the end user, just as fonts and default colors have become for Web users. From the aesthetic point of view, the principle guiding this hope is an old Romantic idea of the art work as an aesthetic unity.

   This principle goes back to the ancient Greek philosopher Aristotle, who with his characteristic common sense announced that a good drama has a beginning, a middle, and an end. In the early nineteenth century, the romantic poet Coleridge wrote that "a work of art contains within itself the reason why it is so and not otherwise." The emphasis in Coleridge's case is on the phrase "in itself": the artwork is free of external constraints, such as the need to serve God or the state, and is beautiful to the extent that it alone determines its own form. This was relatively easy for a period in which the arts—sculpture, painting, poetry, music, and the then new form of the novel—were highly distinct from one another. Later in the same century the composer Wagner attempted the Gesamtkunstwerk, the total artwork, in his case the transformation of opera into "music theatre" combining architecture, performance, poetry, song, and music into a single and overwhelming whole. But even Wagner's fans would admit that in his case, contrary to the other great adage of organic unity, the parts are greater than their sum, and his music is prized far more than his storytelling ability or his poetry. Nonetheless, the idea of a unifying principle that can tie the disparate elements of an artwork together into a whole that is greater than the sum of its parts remains a touchstone, and not only in art.

Designers too have developed a doctrine of unity. The revolution in design in the early twentieth century associated with constructivism in Russia, the Bauhaus in Germany, and de Stijl in Holland is characterized by two principles. First, that form follows function: the shape of a design should be a direct result of its purpose. This was a reaction against the ornate decoration applied by nineteenth-century designers to everything from furniture to machine presses. But it also expresses a belief in the organic relation between the use and the form of an object, the one growing from the other. The second principle is that the elements of a design should all share the same vocabulary of forms. This is most obvious in the work of architects like Frank Lloyd Wright and Mies van der Rohe, who not only designed buildings, but the furniture and even the plumbing and light fittings so that every part of the building echoed the same fundamental form. This extends into contemporary concepts of branding, where a company is reckoned to increase recognition of its identity among the public (and therefore its sales) by ensuring that everything that emanates from it—from packaging to adverts to letterheads—shares a strongly marked brand. Examples would include the Coke logo, IBM's blue, or the iconoclastic redesign of desktop computers which accompanied the relaunch of Apple in the 1990s.

To ensure the same principles of brand identity and of aesthetic unity, Web designers will go to great lengths to provide every distinct page on a Website with a shared appearance. Tools for this unification include the old warhorses like logos and company colors. But they also include new tools such as the use of frames, so that new pages are always framed by a shared menu, and cascading style sheets, which allow the designer to define common properties for all the pages on a site. This principle has worked very well for a number of important Websites. Amazon, Yahoo!, indeed most search engines, CDnow, Netscape, and others among the most commercially successful sites have worked hard to establish and maintain instantly recognizable pages, and logos that can advertise links to them from other

"To ensure the same principles of brand identity and of aesthetic unity, Web designers will go to great lengths to provide every distinct page on a Web-site with a shared appearance." The Crate and Barrel site. http://www .crateandbarrel.com/

sites. Even small organizations can benefit from the maintenance of a strong brand identity on the Web, and for many people it is a simple matter of good taste to prefer the orderly over the random, and the unified over messy mixes of disparate and clashing elements.

An interesting counterexample is Mark Amerika's *Grammatron* site, an experimental hypertext fiction which deliberately thwarts our expectations, trying out new styles and new ways of mixing images, texts, fonts, colors, and sounds on almost every page. Behind this inorganic disunity lies a more recent aesthetic idea critical of organic unity because it either presupposes or produces an illusion of an organically unified self that mirrors the unity of the design. Instead, the fragmentary and dispersed arrangement of elements is intended to mirror a self in a state of crisis, a self that is unanchored by a fixed "I" and has become schizophrenic. For many commentators on contemporary culture, schizophrenia is not an illness afflicting an unfortunate percentage of the population but the very heart of the condition under which we now live.

Amerika's *Grammatron* is an attempt not just to describe that situation of moral uncertainty, political apathy, and nomadic psyches, but to provide an uncertain, angry, confused, and meandering form in which to express it. Like many people in cultural studies, I find this rebellion against order fascinating and attractive. But intellectually, I have to admit that it has a major failing. By opposing order with chaos, information with entropy, unity with schizophrenia, dominance with resistance, Amerika offers his visitors only a reverse image of the orderly universe which he wants to revolt against. It is as if he has taken each rule of "good" design and simply done the opposite. In this way, rather than make something brand new, he has merely produced a shadow of the orderly design to which he opposes himself.

The organic principle, then, still remains intact, even where it has been attacked. However, the concept of conversion media adds a new dimension to the organic unification of Web design. So far I have stressed the audiovisual media familiar from the arts and entertainment worlds. But computing and network communication has a history which involves not only leisure media, but the media of work and war, where both the computer and the Internet were first born. According to the media historian Friedrich Kittler, the computer monitor derives not from television but from the wartime invention of radar in the 1940s, and radar and other technical displays long predate the use of screens on desktop computers or even mainframes. Other historians point toward a series of military and work-related types of presentation. For example, one of the dominant forms of visual representation for the last five hundred years has been the map. Digital maps can combine several types of information and several kinds of display into a single Geographic Information System, using, for example, postal (ZIP) codes, satellite data on land use, census information, and graphic displays of average incomes or purchasing habits at local stores. Some cartographic techniques have strong military origins (the maps of isobars used in weather reports, for example, use nineteenth-century techniques for showing battle lines), while others derive from the use of a huge variety of graphs in scientific and social statistical analysis.

Perhaps the single most significant type of visual display for the history of modern computing is double-entry bookkeeping. It was the invention of spreadsheet software that persuaded so many smaller companies to invest in information technology and company intranets at a time when the market was dominated by massive corporate and military-academic mainframe computers. Spreadsheets, and rather later word processing, offered companies huge savings on skilled and therefore expensive staff. With off-the-shelf software like Lotus 1–2–3, even the smallest company could afford to sack the (male) accountant and employ a cheaper (female) bookkeeper instead. But what we tend to forget is that the spreadsheet is a visual display of financial data, and as a visual medium it too has had an impact, perhaps a bigger one than anything else, on the ways in which computer interfaces have been designed.

One other major medium has also traditionally been excluded from the debates over convergence and conversion, and that is the catalog. Professional researchers in industry and academia probably spend as much time using catalogs, indexes, and bibliographies as they do using the sources they are trying to find. Over the last hundred and fifty years, catalogs have evolved from simple lists of authors and titles to complex devices for information retrieval. The majority of libraries use systems like the Library of Congress standard, which classifies books according to their major subject. More sophisticated information retrieval systems use keywords, so that a book on the treatment of liver disease in South American cattle can be found not only under veterinary science, but also under the anatomy of the liver, beef husbandry, and regional studies. An extension of this system forms the basis for all search engines, the commonest form of interaction we have with the Web. It is important to understand that, for Web surfers, the "catalog" function of search engines is more fundamental than, for example, the storytelling function of popular fiction, news journalism, or film and television narrative. Perhaps this emphasis helps to clarify why I believe *Grammatron* is misguided in setting itself against familiar narrative forms as one of its methods of rebellion: narrative is not that important on the Web. Searching is.

When we add maps, spreadsheets, and catalogs to the list of text, audio, and still and moving images, we not only arrive at a more complex and subtle set of categories for understanding the conversion media; we also have to begin to recognize the powers ranged against the full convergence of media. It is relatively easy to find examples in which text, sound, and image are combined—it happens every night on the TV news. When live-streaming video becomes a possibility, at least in small frames within the page, it will be a commonplace of the Web. Various kinds of graphic display, maps, spreadsheets, and site-specific search engines are also common. What is less common is to find a site in which all these things form a single, organic, unified impression for the end user. Instead, on sites like CNN's news site, the impression is of a hastily constructed notice board cluttered with the fragmented debris of dozens of functions, graphics, and links, with nothing but a logo and a shared root index to hold them together. We may just have to resign ourselves to the schizophrenic aesthetic of a modernity that has become too fast and too complicated for the old ideal of organic unity.

Montage

Among the first people to recognize this new quality of life were the Dadaists, a loose gang of anarchistic artists and intellectuals who shared little but a sense of the pointlessness of European civilization at the height of the trench warfare of World War I. One of them, Max Ernst, would spend much of his life discovering new ways to express, in his early years, the absurdity of culture, and in his later years, the mysteries, secrets, horrors, and delights that lie hidden under its apparent coherence. One of the first artists to use photomontage, he took to cutting up found photographs and reassembling them into ridiculous, frightening new compositions. Later he would compose whole "novels" out of cut-up magazine illustrations of the previous century, or make works by painting over found images to obscure everything but the most bizarre juxtapositions. For Ernst, chance was the key to his art: a way of using random events to shape the finished work.

There are some Websites that use related techniques which, if not entirely random, nonetheless create the conditions for unforeseen and unforeseeable juxtapositions. Simon Biggs's *Great Wall of China*, for example, is a site scripted in Macromedia Director, usually used to author CD-ROMs. The site includes an engine which uses the grammar and vocabulary of a Kafka short story to generate new sentences as the user rolls over or clicks on various elements on the page. The *communimage* project (http://www.communimage.ch), established by expo.01, the Swiss National Exhibition, is a growing patchwork mosaic of over three thousand images provided and positioned by visitors, where the varying motives of each visitor ensure that the relationships between neighboring images are constantly startling. Ernst was a great artist because he used his own reactions to decide which random effects were interesting enough to make public. *The Great Wall of China*, by contrast, allocates that decision to the machine, confronting us with bizarre new sentences that we are left to make sense of or not. The *communimage* project takes yet another tack, effectively employing the actions of visitors as a generator of randomness. So we can see that chance is only one part of the equation: the principle of random juxtaposition requires that the viewer or reader decide which combinations are spooky or illuminating or disturbing.

In fact, by putting my description of Ernst in this chapter just after the sentence about living in a schizophrenic world, I was using a similar technique: making spatial proximity link the two things, rather than logical argument or narrative conventions. This is a relatively easy stunt to achieve in one medium—images or words—but much harder to do across media. Probably the two most famous practitioners of the art of montage, the most common name given to this style of colliding fragments together to make new objects, are the early Russian filmmaker Sergei Eisenstein and the contemporary Swiss director Jean-Luc Godard. Both make a point of making sound and image work across one another, not necessarily synchronized, so that the images comment on the sound and the sound on the images. In Godard's case texts printed onto the film provide a third tool for creating clashes between disparate objects. Both Godard and Eisenstein are politically radical, and both have produced important bodies of theoretical writing on montage. Central to both is the concept of dialectic, which we need to grasp if we are to see how montage attempts to offer a third route to structuring multimedia.

Where hierarchy uses dominance as a way of creating order, and organicism uses a kind of democracy among the media as its principle of harmony, montage can be said to depend upon conflict. Hierarchy and organicism could therefore be seen as essentially conservative, in the sense that they attempt to conserve a sense of propriety and symmetry, and to achieve a still moment of clarity or identity. Montage, however, is about the use of the unexpected to create unthought-of new ideas: it is about change. Dialectics is the philosophical method which concentrates on change, and sees the root of change in contradiction. As this was the chosen analytical method of Karl Marx, there has been an immense literature about dialectics, all of which can be ignored for our purposes, save only that, considered as a dialectic, montage arranges conflicts between image and image, and between image and sound and text. For example, in Godard's film *Two or Three Things I Know about Her* (1966), a whispered conversation about urban regeneration is contrasted with images of urban decay, while pictures of glowing shopping malls are accompanied by the unbearably aggressive noise of pneumatic drills, and all of them are reframed by the introduction of a constantly startling comparison between Paris and a prostitute who lives there, both of whom are the "her" of the title.

A related politicized montage is employed by RTMark, an anonymous tactical media group who achieved notoriety for building an alternative George W. Bush campaign Website. Looking pretty much like the real one, RTMark's site is full of scabrous revelations about campaign funds, previous policy decisions, weird public statements, and miscellaneous scandal. On its own, the site would be merely satirical, but by constantly inviting comparison with Bush's own campaign site, it creates a juxtaposition out of which the audience is invited to create new kinds of meaning. The UK-based Mongrel have likewise produced a guerrilla site (http://www.mongrel.co.uk) which takes pages from corporate Websites and remakes them in order to pose embarrassing questions about race and racism. Again, it is the contradiction between the official and the unofficial that makes the new site important: if there were no British Airways site, there would be no point in creating an antagonistic mirror to it.

But perhaps the best-known and most profoundly dialectical site is that run by Jodi, two Dutch artists based in Barcelona. Over the several years that I have been visiting it, www.jodi.org has rarely looked the same twice, so descriptions will of necessity be inaccurate. But then, that is part of the site's strategy: to provide a constant reminder of the ephemerality of all digital media, especially on the Web. The site frequently uses images we associate with lost connections, error codes, and crashes, the constant underbelly of Web culture. Just as the invention of the railway is also the invention of the railway disaster so, they seem to say, the invention of the computer is the invention of data crash. "Error 404" is a constant refrain—the error message set up by the Web to indicate an incorrect address or a refusal from a server: whenever you call, Jodi are not at home. You will frequently find whole pages of apparently meaningless ASCII script blinking randomly, or scraps of Java script that not only cause apparently random screen events but also make bogus Java error screens pop up in your browser. On a bad day, a visit will crash your browser, even your whole system.

One of the fascinating things about Jodi is that it is clearly written by gifted programmers for whom the spirit of medium-specificity is still important. Their canvases are network computers, their brushes high-level computer languages, and much of the content of their work is a satire on Web culture. Where the commercialization of the Web is marketed on information, Jodi are interested in the space of contradiction between information and entropy, order and chaos. The dialectical principle comes from their refusal to take the option of being prochaos. Instead, they work at the border between meaning and meaninglessness, where the contradictions between the invisibly small, unthinkably fast traffic in zeros and ones and the slow download of image-heavy pages, for example, can be explored. Users can decide for themselves whether to read this as an allegory of the global information economy, too vast for anyone to understand, let alone control, or a commentary on the relationship between culture and anarchy, or an ecological parable, or a philosophical statement. When a "mailto" button produces a letter form that automatically fills up with the "Good News" virus spam (the warning against a supposed virus carried an email headed "Good News" that has been circulating at least since 1995), there is a direct comment on the relation between freedom and determination on the Web. But the spam is also a reminder that surfing the Jodi site feels constantly risky, as though the safety net of clean, comprehensible design had been taken away, and the ever-present but usually forgotten power of viruses is forced into consciousness. So the site constantly attracts you with its novelty, its wit, and its visual flair (drawing on the widest possible range of imagery from icons to drop-down menus, error codes to self-generating maps of current Web use). But at the same time it pushes you away with the sense of risk, that you might be endangering your own machine by linking it to this site.

Jodi then uses dialectical methods of montage to make us aware of a dialectical process of order and entropy in the Web as a whole. And at the same time, it creates a dialectical relation with its visitors, alternately attracting and repelling them, inviting you to recognize the iconography of the fashionably Web-savvy, then baffling you with cues for interaction that deliberately fail to respond to your actions. The Jodi Website is an invaluable corrective to the hierarchical and organic types of site. On the other hand, it has to be said that this is a site where style triumphs over content: this is not a data-rich site in any ordinary sense of the word, although I would argue that it is just as valuable, and perhaps more so, than any content-oriented site I know.

Many other sites use montage principles to create entertaining, weird, or scary experiences for their visitors, some of them to quite remarkable effect, such as the Website for the Museum of Jurassic Technology. The cut-and-paste aesthetic of computer applications makes montage and collage (Picasso's variation on the technique, from the French word for glue) the most natural of games with the new technology. And while the first law of thermodynamics says that energy can neither be created nor destroyed, the same is not true about information Montage, including both political and random variants, acts like mutation in biological organisms, as a way of creating unique and perhaps invaluable new creations that can enrich and enlighten our cultures. But on the other hand, there is a risk that montage might become a cliché, or a technique with all the panache and originality of drawing mustaches on posters.

In the widely read introduction to his book *The Order of Things*, the historian and philosopher Michel Foucault drew attention to the passion modern societies show for cataloging and classifying. Our problem is that there is too much information, and we must spend a certain amount of time organizing it in order for it to have any use. But every technique we devise for creating lists relies on decisions about categories that can be controversial or even misleading—think of all those catalogs which depend on the name of the author, and look at Russell

Potter's chapter "Authorship," in this volume. Books are hard enough to catalog: the poor slide librarian is a member of an international community who have been striving to find a workable taxonomy (or list of types) for photography for decades. And yet the catalog, however we decide to organize it, has one great feature: it is a machine for creating new juxtapositions. Almost any search engine will demonstrate this fact: a search for "stocks," for example, will bring you the medieval punishment as well as Wall Street brokers: a whole new meaning to the phrase "stock market." Almost any kind of list will bring together odd combinations. But do they mean anything to us? And do they really add anything new to the stock of culture?

Accidents are part and parcel of the digital culture, all the more so in the immense bazaar of images and ideas which is the Internet. And since digital media are media of transformation as well as of storage and communication, it should come as no surprise that we have become a cybernation of montagists. But are we doing anything other than messing around in a vast, planetary archive? All our narratives about the role of chance in science and discovery—the vulcanization of rubber, the discovery of penicillin—involve people who knew what they were looking for, and recognized what it was when it presented itself to them. The problem of montage as a principle of multimedia design is that it can be undertaken without a sense of what we are looking for or how to recognize success when it arrives. The result is what cultural critics call pastiche, in which elements are brought together which have no relationship with one another (pastiche is therefore linked to the loss of shared values in contemporary society, values that would otherwise produce meaningful relationships between disparate objects).

The greatest risk of the montage principle is that it can lose its central contradiction: the contradiction between the montage and its reader. Montage depends on shock, and that in turn depends on the reader having expectations that can be overturned. But if we have no expectations there can be no surprises, and therefore no contradiction between the montage and the ordinary. Without a principle of contradiction, montage becomes pastiche, and once again merely confirms the scattered and dispersed relationships between the elements of multimedia, not their integration into a single, unified practice. Montage may have been the royal road to new meanings in the twentieth century, but in the twenty-first, either because our whole culture is already contradictory, or because the principle of contradiction has been lost in the vast mosaic of clashing cultural emblems, montage may no longer have the power to illuminate. A commercial for a family car that uses eighteenth- century music hasn't created a new kind of meaning: it has dissolved old associations and failed to replace them with anything else.

A clear sense of what this might mean can be discovered at the *Landfill* site (http://www.potatoland.com/landfill) where visitors are invited to dump unwanted Web pages. A special microprogram then treats the incoming code as if it were compost, and the visitor is treated to a massive file of decomposing HTML and fragmenting images rendered out of the files people have dumped there. *Landfill* suggests that there might be some future use for all that junk code—as fertilizer for new generations, or as a new territory built out onto the emptier reaches of cyberspace on which new dwellings can be constructed. But the overwhelming impression is of an indigestible morass of data and its impossible diversity. Though it wants to create a dialectic of decay and construction, *Landfill* can suggest instead that the sheer number of elements can no longer be brought into a meaningful whole, even as contradictions, and that we are condemned to inhabit an archive without a catalog.

Back to the Future

We can see then that three of the most widely used principles for drawing media together into single hybrid forms have major flaws when they are employed in the digital world of the Web. One of my favorite responses to this problem comes in the form of an alternative browser, *Webstalker* (downloadable free at http://backspace.org/iod/). *Webstalker* connects you to the Internet in a new way. Instead of displaying all the graphics and texts, one window shows you nothing but the scrolling HTML code that underlies the pages. Meanwhile a second window (you draw, scale, and allocate functions to the windows yourself) draws a map of the Internet starting from the first URL you enter. Making its map in real time, *Webstalker* ignores the apparent content of pages in favor of the raw content of code and the principle of connectivity. This makes it a wonderful tool for analyzing the structure of Websites and their degree of connectedness with the

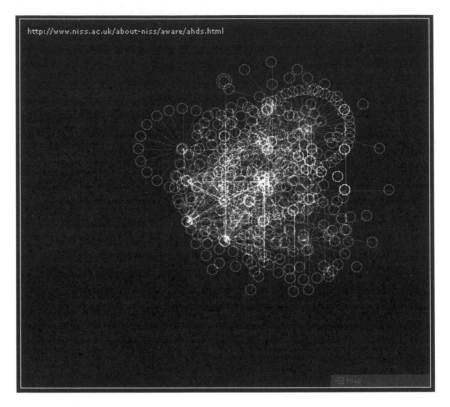

http://www.niss.ac.uk/about-niss/aware/ahds.html

"*Webstalker* ignores the apparent content of pages in favor of the raw content of code and the principle of connectivity." The Webstalker site. http://www
.backspace.org/iod/iod4.html

rest of the Web. Left to run for sufficient time, it will draw a map of vast areas of the Web. One aspect of the software is particularly interesting in the context of convergence and conversion: the way it prioritizes connectivity.

In the discussion so far, I have concentrated on only one aspect of Web traffic: the Web as a publication medium. But of course the other family of media involved in the Web comprises the whole field of telecommunications. In some ways the Web is no different from previous media, except that it has that single magical tool, the hyperlink. But in other ways, the Web also draws on a history of communications from the telegraph to cellular phones and satellite telephony, a history of two-way communication. Trade exhibitions in 1999 were already demonstrating two-way cellular video telephony: the promise of high-bandwidth domestic connections to the Web may well bring this new form of interaction into widespread use, and be as popular as, for example, net.radio has already been, and perhaps more so. This interconnectivity multiplies the power of hyperlinks by the ability to interact provided by telecommunications, bringing another degree of complexity to the existing mix of graphic, textual, audio, and visual media.

But it also brings with it an added degree of complexity to the problem that taxed us at the beginning of this chapter, namely, the problem of control over the end user's experience. The tendency to use powerful software packages to determine the appearance of pages in users' browser windows is increasingly apparent today, especially among image-conscious promoters of brand identities. At the same time, however, the promised new bandwidth of fiber optics and low Earth orbit satellites suggests that users can begin to expect a higher degree of interaction, and therefore a greater input into the content of Web pages. One possible upshot of this state of affairs might be complete chaos; another might be a golden age of media democracy. But we also need to be aware that if the power is shifting from Web authors to Web audiences, then audiences must accept, along with the right to interact, the responsibilities that have always fallen on the shoulders of authors. Alternatively, or perhaps simultaneously, we must also realize that interactive content is ephemeral. Not only does the Web loosen the author's grip on the final spatial layout of the page; digital technologies mean that its content is also open to change, and if to change, then to disappearance. Older media aimed for a certain kind of permanence, even in the case of performance arts like theater and dance. Web media, on the other hand, are by definition malleable, fragile, and evanescent.

We tend to think of the Web in terms of a sort of virtual geography: cyberspace. (See "Cyberspace," this volume.) But the problem of multimedia brings us to another dimension of Web communication: cybertime. Even the swiftest connections bring in the elements of a page in a definite order, and some elements occupy a time scale whole orders of magnitude greater or smaller than others, readily observable when downloading an MP3 or video file. We should add to such technical time scales the vital commodity for which so many Websites compete: the end user's time. There are no easy answers to the problems of multimedia, but the temporal aspect does raise at least one intriguing thought. Perhaps we should not be looking forward to faster and faster connections, but to slower and slower contemplation of what we have already downloaded. That way, perhaps we can pay a little more attention to the meanings created by linking from one page to another. The majority of sites still link pages by traditional print criteria based on linear argument, narrative, or the use of indexes. But perhaps we need to slow down just enough to consider the meaning of linkage itself—between pages, between sites, and between media. Perhaps then we can put ourselves in a frame of mind that will allow us to invent new ways of making the disparate media of Web culture combine to produce new harmonies or new contradictions.

Bibliography

Introduction

Horner, Bruce, and Thomas Swiss, eds. 1999. *Key Terms for Popular Music and Culture*. Malden, Mass. Blackwell.

Moulthop, Stuart. 1997. "Pushing Back: Living and Writing in Broken Space." *Modern Fiction Studies* 43 (3):651–674. http://muse.jhu.edu/journals/modern_fiction_studies/

Ross, Andrew. 1998. *Real Love*. New York: New York University Press.

Williams, Raymond. 1976. *Keywords: A Vocabulary of Culture and Society*. New York: Oxford University Press.

Chapter 1. Community

Armstrong, A., and J. Hagel. 1997. *Net Gain*. Cambridge: Harvard Business School Press.

Brand, S. 1974. *Cybernetic Frontiers*. New York: Random House.

Dibbell, J. December 21, 1993. "A Rape in Cyberspace." *Village Voice*, 375–395.

Figallo, C. 1998. *Hosting Web Communities: Building Relationships, Increasing Customer Loyalty, and Maintaining a Competitive Edge*. New York: John Wiley.

Gelder, L.S. October 1985. "The Strange Case of the Electronic Lover." *Ms.*, 94–95

Hafner, K. 1997. May. "The Epic Sage of The Well." *Wired*, 5:05.

Levy, S. 1984. *Hackers*. New York: Dell Publishing.

Reno v ACLU 521 U.S. 844. (1977) U.S. LEXIS 4037, section VII.

Rheingold, H. 1993. *The Virtual Community: Homesteading on the Electronic Frontier*. Reading, Mass.: Addison-Wesley.

Sardar, Z. 1996. "alt.civilizations.faq: Cyberspace as the Darker Side of the West." In *Cyberfutures: Culture and Politics on the Information Superhighway*, ed. Ziauddin Sardar and J. R. Ravetz, 14–41. New York: New York University Press.

Slavoj Žižek. 1997. *The Plague of Fantasies*. London: Verso.

Stoll, C. 1995. *Silicon Snake Oil: Second Thoughts on the Information Highway.* New York: Doubleday.

Stone, Allucquere Rosanne. 1995. *The War of Desire and Technology at the Close of the Mechanical Age.* Cambridge: MIT Press.

Chapter 2. Identity

Barlow, John Perry. 1996. "A Cyberspace Independence Declaration" www .eff.org/pub/Publications/John_Perry_Barlow/barlow_0296. declaration

Bolter, Jay David, and Richard Grusin. 1999. *Remediation: Understanding New Media.* Cambridge: MIT Press.

Bolter, Jay David. 2000. *Writing Space: The Computer, Hypertext, and the History of Writing.* 2d ed. Hillsdale, N.J.: Lawrence Earlbaum.

Bruckman, Amy S. 1999. "Gender Swapping on the Internet." In *CyberReader,* ed. Victor J. Vitanza, 418–424. 2d ed. Needham, Heights, Mass.: Allyn and Bacon.

Eisenstein, Elizabeth. 1979. *The Printing Press as an Agent of Change.* 2 vols. Cambridge: Cambridge University Press.

Gergen, Kenneth. 1991. *The Saturated Self: Dilemmas of Identity in Contemporary Life.* New York: Basic Books.

Joyce, Michael. 1995. *Of Two Minds: Hypertext Pedagogy and Poetics.* Ann Arbor: University of Michigan Press.

Stone, Allucquere Roseanne. 1991. "Will the Real Body Please Stand Up? Boundary Stories about Virtual Cultures." In *Cyberspace: First Steps,* ed. Michael Benedikt, 81–118. Cambridge: MIT Press.

Turkle, Sherry. 1995. *Life on the Screen: Identity in the Age of the Internet.* New York: Simon and Schuster.

Chapter 3. Gender

Balsamo, Anne. 1996. *Technologies of the Gendered Body: Reading Cyborg Women.* Durham, N.C.: Duke University Press.

Baring, Anne, and Jules Cashford. [1991] 1993. *The Myth of the Goddess: Evolution of an Image.* New York: Viking. 2d ed. by London: Penguin-Arkana.

Berger, Maurice et al., eds. 1995. *Constructing Masculinity.* New York: Routledge.

Bornstein, Kate. 1994. *Gender Outlaw: On Men, Women, and the Rest of Us.* London: Routledge.

———. "A Transgender Transsexual Postmodern Tiresias." http://www .ctheory.com/a-kate_bornstein.html

Butler, Judith. 1990. *Gender Trouble: Feminism and the Subversion of Identity.* New York: Routledge.

————. 1993. *Bodies that Matter: On the Discursive Limits of "Sex."* New York: Routledge.

Cherny, Lynn, and Elizabeth Reba Wise, eds. 1996. *wired_women.* Toronto: Seal Press. Cybergender and Techgender http://vos.ucsb.edu/shuttle/gender.html#cyber

Davis-Floyd, Robbie, and Joseph Dumit, eds. 1998. *Cyborg Babies: From Techno-Sex to Techno-Tots.* New York: Routledge.

de Lauretis, Teresa. 1987. *Technologies of Gender.* Bloomington: Indiana University Press.

————. 1994. *The Practice of Love.* Bloomington: Indiana University Press.

Epstein, Julia, and Kristine Straub, eds. 1991. *Body Guards: The Cultural Politics of Gender Ambiguity.* New York: Routledge.

Garber, Marjorie. 1992. *Vested Interests: Cross-Dressing and Cultural Anxiety.* New York: Routledge.

Gibson, William. 1984. *Neuromancer.* New York: Ace Books.

Halberstam, Judith, and Ira Livingston, eds. 1995. Posthuman Bodies. Bloomington: Indiana University Press.

Haraway, Donna. 1991. *Simians, Cyborgs and Women: The Reinvention of Nature.* New York: Routledge.

————. 1996. *Modest_Witness@Second_Millenium.FemaleMan_Meets_OncoMouse: Feminism and Technoscience.* New York: Routledge.

Herdt, Gilbert H., ed. 1993. *Third Sex, Third Gender: Beyond Sexual Dimorphism in Culture and History.* New York: Zone Books.

Lawley, Elizabeth Lane. "Computers and the Communication of Gender." http://www.itcs.com/elawley/gender.html

Leeson, Lynn Hershman, ed. 1996. *Clicking In: Hot Links to a Digital Culture.* Seattle: Bay Press.

Morse, Margaret. 1998. *Virtualities: Television, Media Art, and Cyberculture.* Bloomington: Indiana University Press.

Ross, Andrew, and Constance Penley, eds. 1991. *Technoculture.* Minneapolis: University of Minnesota Press.

"Sex, Identity and the Homepage." *Babes on the Web.* http://www.newcastle .edu.au/department/so/babes.htm. Reprinted from *Media International Australia.* May 1997:84, 39–45.

Stone, Allucquere Roseanne. 1991. "Will the Real Body Please Stand Up? Boundary Stories about Virtual Cultures." In *Cyberspace: First Steps*, ed. Michael Benedikt, 81–118. Cambridge: MIT Press.

————. 1995. *The War of Desire and Technology at the Close of the Mechanical Age.* Cambridge: MIT University Press.

Terry, Jennifer, and Melodie Calvert, eds. 1997. *Processed Lives: Gender and Technology in Everyday Life.* London: Routledge.

Turkle, Sherry. [1995] 1997. *Life on the Screen: Identity in the Age of the Internet.* New York: Simon and Schuster.

Chapter 4. Race

Anzaldúa, G. 1987. *Borderlands/La Frontera*. San Francisco: Aunt Lute Books.

Bakhtin, M. 1981. *The Dialogic Imagination*. Austin: University of Texas Press.

Hoffman, D., and Novak W. February 2, 1998, on-line. "Bridging the Digital Divide: The Impact of Race on Computer Access and Internet Use." (Working Paper). This article is a longer version of their article "Bridging the Racial Divide on the Internet," published in *Science*, April 17, 1998.

Kolko, B., L. Nakamura, and G. Rodman, eds. 1999. *Race in Cyberspace*. New York: Routledge.

Nakamura, L. Victor J. Vitanza ed. 1999. "Race in/for Cyberspace: Racial Passing and Identity Tourism." In *CyberReader*, ed. Victor J. Vitanza. 2d ed., 49–59. Needham Heights, Mass.: Allyn and Bacon.

Poster, M. 1995. *The Second Media Age*. Cambridge: Polity Press.

Radcliff, D. April 18, 1999. "Biz Careers: Champions of Women in Technology." *Computer world*. on-line. http://www.computerworld.com/home/features.nsf/all/990118women

Sterne, J. 1999. "The Computer Race Meets Computer Classes: How Computers in Schools Helped Shape the Racial Topography of the Internet." In *Race in Cyberspace*, ed. B. Kolko, L. Nakamura, and G. Rodman, 179–184. New York: Routledge.

Turkle, S. 1997. *Life on the Screen: Identity in the Age of the Internet*. New York: Touchstone.

Zickmund, S. 1997. "Approaching the Radical Other: The Discursive Culture of Cyberhate." In *Virtual Culture: Identity and Communication in Cybersociety*, ed. Steven G. Jones, 185–205 London: Sage.

Chapter 5. Political Economy

Auletta, K. August 16, 1999. "Hard Core." *New Yorker Magazine* 41–69.

DuBoff, R. 1984. "The Rise of Communication Regulation: The Telegraph Industry, 1844–1880." *Journal of Communication*, 3: 34, 52–66.

Gates, B., with Norman C. Myhrvold and Peter Rinearson. 1995. *The Road Ahead*. New York: Viking.

Harris, W. B. April 1957. "The Electronic Business." *Fortune*, 137–226.

Johnson, S. October 23, 1997. "Metaphor Monopoly." *New York Times*, A27.

Lohr, S., and J. Markoff. October 8 1998. "Microsoft's World." *New York Times*, A1.

McChesney, R. W. 1999. *Rich Media, Poor Democracy*. Urbana: University of Illinois Press.

Mosco. V. 1996. *The Political Economy of Communication*. London: Sage.

NetAction: http://www.netaction.org

Noble, D. *Digital Diploma Mills*. http://www.journet.com/twu/diplomamills .html

Robins, K., and F. Webster. 1999. *Times of the Technoculture*. New York: Routledge.

Schiller, D. 1999. *Digital Capitalism*. Cambridge: MIT Press.

Wertheim, M. 1999. *The Pearly Gates of Cyberspace*. New York: W. W. Norton.

Chapter 6. Cyberspace

Benedikt, M. 1992. *Cyberspace: First Steps*. Cambridge: MIT Press.

Boyer, M Christine. 1996. *Cybercities*. New York: Princeton Architectural Press.

DiGiacomo, Kristen. January 25, 1999. Cyberspace newsgroup posting. http://www.cshore.com/sapief/cgi-bin/classbd/messages/31.html)

Druckrey, T. n.d. "Panorama to Globarama." Accessed December 2, 1999. http://www.venge.com/panoram.html

Gans, D. and Goffman, K. 1990. Interview with Mitch Kapor and John Barlow. Originally published in *Wired* (September). http://eff.bilkent.edu.tr/ pub/Publications/John_Perry_Barlow/HTML/barlow_and_kapor_in_ wired_interview.html

Gibson, William. 1984. *Neuromancer*. New York: Ace Books.

Jameson, F. 1984. "Postmodernism or the Cultural Logic of Late Capitalism." *New Left Review*, 146:53–93.

Lefebvre, H. 1972. *Le Droit à la ville*. Paris: Anthropos.

———. 1991. *The Production of Space*. Trans. H. Nicholson-Smith. Oxford: Basil Blackwell.

Luke, Carmen. 1996. "ekstasis@cyberia." Graduate School of Education, University of Queensland. Originally published in *Discourse*, 17 (2):187–208. http://www.gseis.ucla.edu/courses/ed253a/Luke/CYBERDIS.html

Negroponte, Nicholas. 1998. "Back Page." Originally published in *Wired*, 6:12. http://nicholas.www.media.mit.edu/people/nicholas/Wired/WIRED6– 12.html

Nunes, Mark. 1995. "Baudrillard in Cyberspace: Internet, Virtuality, and Postmodernity." DeKalb College. Originally published in *Style*, 29:314–327. http://www.dc.peachnet.edu/~mnunes/jbnet.html

Sardar, Ziauddin, and J. R. Ravetz, eds. 1996. *Cyberfutures: Culture and Politics on the Information Superhighway*. New York: New York University Press.

Shields, R. 1999. *Lefebvre, Love and Struggle: Spatial Dialectics*. London: Routledge.
———. forthcoming. "Hypertext Links: The Ethic of the Index and its Space-Time Effects." In *The World Wide Web: Metaphor, Magic and Power*, ed. T. Swiss and A. Herman. New York: Routledge.

Stone, Allucquere Roseanne. 1995. *The War of Desire and Technology at the Close of the Mechanical Age*. Cambridge, MA: MIT Press.

Todorov, Tzvetan. 1984. *The Conquest of America*. New York: Harper and Row.

Virillio, Paul. August 1995. "Speed and Information: Cyberspace Alarm!" *Ctheory* [On-line journal], 30. http://www.ctheory.com/a30–cyberspace_alarm.html. Originally published in French in *Le monde diplomatique*. August 1995.

Chapter 7. Governance

Beck, Ulrich. 1992. *Risk Society: Towards a New Modernity*. London: Sage.

Castells, Manuel. 1996–1998. *The Information Age: Economy, Society, and Culture*, 3 vols. Oxford: Blackwell.

Davidson, James Dale, and Lord William Rees-Mogg. 1997. *The Sovereign Individual: How to Survive and Thrive during the Collapse of the Welfare State*. New York: Simon and Schuster.

Deibert, Ronald, J. 1997. *Parchment, Printing, and Hypermedia: Communication in World Order Transformation*. New York: Columbia University Press.

Dizard, Wilson, Jr. 1997. *MegaNet: How the Global Communications Network Will Connect Everyone on Earth*. Boulder: Westview Press.

Foucault, Michel. 1979. *Discipline and Punish: The Birth of the Prison*. New York: Vintage.
———. 1980. *The History of Sexuality, Vol. 1: An Introduction*. New York: Vintage.
———. 1991. *The Foucault Effect: Studies in Governmentality*, ed. Graham Burchell, Colin Gordon, and Peter Miller. Chicago: University of Chicago Press.

Gates, Bill, with Norman C. Myhrvold and Peter Rinearson. 1995. *The Road Ahead*. New York: Viking.

Hirsh, Michael. March 9, 1998. "The Fed's Case against Bill Gates." *Newsweek*, 131 (10):42–43.

Jones, Stephen G., ed. 1993. *Cybersociety: Computer-Mediated Communication and Community*. London: Sage.

Levy, Stephen. March 9, 1998. "Microsoft vs. the World." *Newsweek*, 131 (10):36–42.

Lewis, T. G. 1997. *The Friction-Free Economy: Marketing Strategies for a Wired World*. New York: HarperCollins.

Luke, Timothy W. 1989. *Screens of Power: Ideology, Domination, and Resistance in Informational Society*. Urbann: University of Illinois Press.

————. 1998. "The Politics of Digital Inequality: Access, Capability, and Distribution in Cyberspace." In *The Politics of Cyberspace*, ed. Chris Toulouse and Timothy W. Luke, 121–144. New York: Routledge.

Lyotard, Jean-Francois. 1984. *The Postmodern Condition: A Report on Knowledge*. Minneapolis: University of Minnesota Press.

Madden, Andrew P. April 1998. "The Lawgiver." *Red Herring*, 53:64–69.

Negroponte, Nicholas. 1995. *Being Digital*. New York: Knopf.

Ohmae, Kenichi. 1990. *The Borderless World: Power and Strategy in the Interlinked Economy*. New York: Harper and Row.

Rushkoff, Douglas. 1994. *Cyberia: Life in the Trenches of Hyperspace*. San Francisco: HarperCollins.

Seabrook, John. 1997. *Deeper: Adventures on the Net*. New York: Simon and Schuster.

Wilke, John R., and David Bank. March 4, 1998. "Microsoft Chief Concedes Hardball Tactics." *Wall Street Journal*, B1, B5.

Chapter 8. Ideology

Baudrillard, J. 1988. *The Ecstasy of Communication*. New York: Semiotext(e).

————. 1996. *The Perfect Crime*. New York: Verso.

Deibert, R. J. 1997. *Parchment, Printing, and Hypermedia: Communication in New World Order Transformation*. New York: Columbia University Press.

Fiske, J., and J. Hartley. 1978. *Reading Television*. New York: Methuen.

Gunkel, D., and A. H. Gunkel. 1997. "Virtual Geographies: The New Worlds of Cyberspace." *Critical Studies in Mass Communication*, 14:123–137.

Havelock, E. A. 1986. *The Muse Learns to Write: Reflections on Orality*. New Haven: Yale University Press.

Kavanagh, J. H. 1990. "Ideology." In *Critical Terms for Literary Study*, ed. F. Lentricchia and T. McLaughlin, 59. Chicago: University of Chicago Press.

McLuhan, M. 1964. *Understanding Media: The Extensions of Man*. New York: McGraw-Hill.

Ong, W. 1982. *Orality and Literacy: The Technologizing of the Word*. New York: Routledge.

Swiss, T. 2000. "Jewel Case: Pop Stars, Poets, the Press." In *Pop and the Press: Journalism, Criticism, Popular Music*, ed. S. Jones, 107–117. Philadelphia: Temple University Press.

Chapter 9. Performance

Austin, J. L. 1975. *How to Do Things with Words*. Cambridge: Harvard Univeristy Press.

Balsamo, A. 1996. *Technologies of the Gendered Body: Reading Cyborg Women.* Durham, N.C.: Duke University Press.

Barber, L. 1970. "Interview with J. G. Ballard," *Re/Search* 8/9:157-158.

Bell, M. 1997. "Functions of Performance in Technological-Spectacular Culture." Unpublished paper, Western Washington University, Wash.

Benedikt, M., ed. 1991. *Cyberspace: First Steps.* Cambridge: MIT Press.

Bukatman, S. 1993. *Terminal Identity: The Virtual Subject in Postmodern Science Fiction.* Durham, N.C.: Duke University Press.

Butler, J. 1993. *Bodies That Matter: On the Discursive Limits of "Sex."* New York: Routledge.

Case, S. 1996. *The Domain Matrix: Performing Lesbian at the End of Print Culture.* Bloomington: Indiana University Press.

CNET.COM Web page. October 9, 1995. "Survival Research Laboratories Mad Genius Mark Pauline Hosts Sickening Episodes of Devastation and Pleasure." Posted to Reviews: Best of the Web (art), accessed via http://www.CNET.COM.

Dery, M., ed. 1994. *Flame Wars: The Discourse of Cyberculture.* Durham, N.C.: Duke University Press.

————. 1996. *Escape Velocity: Cyberculture at the End of the Century.* New York: Grove Press.

————. 1997. "Sex Drive." *21.C: Scanning the Future.* 24:40-51.

Diamond, E., ed. 1996. *Performance and Cultural Politics.* New York: Routledge.

Dibbell, J. 1994. "A Rape in Cyberspace; or How an Evil Clown, a Haitian Trickster, Two Wizards, and a Cast of Dozens Turned a Database into a Society." In *Flame Wars: The Discourse of Cyberculture,* ed. Mark Dery. Durham, N.C.: Duke University Press.

Gumbrecht, H. U., and K. L. Pfeiffer, eds. 1994. *Materialities of Communication.* Stanford: Stanford University Press.

Haraway, D. J. 1991. *Simians, Cyborgs, and Women: The Reinvention of Nature.* New York: Routledge.

Jameson, F. 1991. *Postmodernism or, the Culture Logic of Late Capitalism.* Durham, N.C.: Duke University Press.

Jones, S. G., ed. 1997. *Virtual Culture: Identity and Communication in Cybersociety.* London: Sage.

Laurel, B. 1991. *Computers as Theatre.* New York: Addison-Wesley.

Laurel, B., R. Strickland, and R. Tow, with Interval Research Corporation. 1994. "Placeholder: Landscape and Narrative in Virtual Environments." Posted on the Placeholder Web site, accessed via http://www.interval.com/projects/placeholder/Hypertext/Papers/Papers_1.html.

Laurel, B., and R. Tow. 1994. "Placeholder: Real Bodies in Virtual Worlds." Posted on the Placeholder Web site, accessed via http://www.interval.com/projects/placeholder/Hypertext/Papers/Papers_1.html.

Murray, J. H. 1997. *The Future of Narrative in Cyberspace*. New York: Free Press.

Parker, A., and E. K. Sedgwick, eds. 1995. *Performativity and Performance*. New York: Routledge.

Pauline, M. 1994. "Survival Research Laboratories Performs in Austria." In *Flame Wars: The Discourse of Cyberculture*, 287-295. Durham, N.C.: Duke University Press.

————. 1995. Survival Research Laboratories official Web site, accessed via www.srl.org.

Seltzer, M. 1992. *Bodies and Machines*. New York: Routledge.

Springer, C. 1996. *Electronic Eros: Bodies and Desire in the Postindustrial Age*. Austin: University of Texas Press.

Stone, A. R. 1991. "Will the Real Body Please Stand Up? Boundary Stories about Virtual Cultures." In *Cyberspace: First Steps*, ed. M. Benedikt, 81-118. Cambridge: MIT Press.

————. 1995. *The War of Desire and Technology at the Close of the Mechanical Age*. Cambridge: MIT Press.

Strickland, R. February 1994. "Capturing the Sense of a Place." Posted on the Placeholder Web site, accessed via http://interval.com/projects/placeholder/Papers/Papers/1_html.

Virilio, P. 1995. *The Art of the Motor*. Trans. J. Rose. Minneapolis: University of Minnesota Press.

Worthen, W. B. October 1998. "Drama, Performativity, and Performance." *PMLA*, 113 (5):1093-1107.

Chapter 10. Hypertext

Aarseth, Espen. 1997. *Cybertext: Perspectives on Ergodic Literature*. Baltimore: Johns Hopkins University Press. alt.hypertext [newsgroup].

Alt-X Publishing Network. http://www.altx.com

Bolter, Jay David. 1990. *Writing Space: The Computer, Hypertext, and the History of Writing*. Hillsdale, N.J.: Lawrence Erlbaum.

Drucker, Johanna. 1998. *Figuring the Word: Essays on Books, Writing, and Visual Poetics*. New York: Granary Books.

Eastgate Systems. http://www.eastgate.com/

Joyce, Michael. 1995. *Of Two Minds: Hypertext Pedagogy and Poetics*. Ann Arbor: University of Michigan Press.

Kirschenbaum, Matthew G. *Lucid Mapping and Codex Transformissions in the Z-Buffer*. http://www.iath.virginia.edu/~mgk3k/lucid/

Landow, George P. 1997. *Hypertext 2.0*. Baltimore: Johns Hopkins University Press.

McCaffery, Steve, and bpNichol. 1992. *Rational Geomancy: The Kids of the Book-Machine*. Vancouver: Talonbooks.

Nelson, Theodore H. 1981. *Literary Machines*. Swarthmore, Pa.: Self-published.

Nyce, James M., and Paul Kahn. 1991. *From Memex to Hypertext: Vannevar Bush and the Mind's Machine*. Boston: Academic Press.

Origins of a Browser: A Netscape Time Capsule. http://www.eng.buffalo.edu/~clau/mozilla/

Postmodern Culture. http://www.iath.virginia.edu/pmc/

Shumate, Michael. "Hyperizons: Hypertext Fiction." http://www.duke.edu/~mshumate/hyperfic.html

W3history: The History of the World-Wide Web. http://www.w3history.org/

Chapter 11. Narrative

Brigham, Linda. Email correspondence, 06:28 PM 8/18/99 –0500.

Coover, Robert. June 21, 1992. "The End of Books." *The New York Times Book Review*, 11: 23–25.

Dennett, Daniel. 1991. *Consciousness Explained*. Boston: Little Brown.

Harris, Paul. Summer 1999. "Harry Mathews' Al Gore Rhythms." *the electronic book review*: http:www.altx.com/ebr.

Krapp, Peter. 1996. "Derrida On-line." *Oxford Literary Review* 18.1–2:159–174.

Landow, ed. 1994. *Hyper/Text/Theory*. Baltimore: Johns Hopkins University Press.

Mathews, Harry. 1997. *The Journalist*. Normal, Ill.: Dalkey Archive Press.

Nelson, Theodor. 1987. *Literary Machines: The Report on, and of, Project Xanadu*. South Michigan.

———. 1995. "The Transclusion Paradigm." Project Xanadu/Sapporo Hyperlab.

Paulson, William. 1987. "The Literary Canon in the Age of Its Technological Obsolescence." In *Reading Matters: Narrative in the New Media Ecology*, ed. Joseph Tabbi and Michael Wutz, 49-62. Ithaca, N.Y.: Cornell University Press.

Rettberg, Scott, et al. *The Unknown*: http://www.soa.uc.edu/user/unknown.

Strickland, Stephanie. Spring 1997. "Poetry in the Electronic Environment." *the electronic book review*: http://www.altx.com/ebr/ebr5/strick.htm

Tabbi, Joseph. Fall 1997. "Solitary Inventions: David Markson at the End of the Line." In "Technocriticism and Hypernarrative," ed. Katherine Hayles. *Modern Fiction Studies*, 43:745–772.

Wittig, Rob. "The Golden Age of Correspondence." *Tank 20*.

———. Rude Trip: http://www.mcs.net/~ittielli/rudetrip

Chapter 12. Authorship

Barthes, Ronald. 1977. "The Death of the Author." In *Image, Music, Text*, ed. and trans. Stephen Heath, 57-71. New York: Hill.

Copyright Clearance Center (CCC): http://www.copyright.com

Foucault, Michel. 1980. "What Is an Author?" In *Language, Counter-Memory, Practice*. Ithaca: Cornell University Press.

Goodnoise.com: http://www.goodnoise.com

Liquid Audio: http://www.liquidaudio.com

New York Times Cybertimes Copyright Issues Page http://www.nytimes.com/library/tech/reference/index-copyright.html

Public Enemy Homepage: http://www.publicenemy.com

Silverman, Kenneth. 1992. *Edgar A. Poe: Mournful and Never-Ending Remembrance*. New York: Harper Perennial.

Visual Arts Copyright Resources: http://www.vra.oberlin.edu/copyright.html

Chapter 13. Multimedia

Bolter, J. D., and Grusin R. 1999. *Remediation: Understanding New Media*. Cambridge: MIT Press.

Gere, C. 1999. "Hypermedia and Emblematics." In *Computing and Visual Culture: Representation and Interpretation. Fourteenth Annual CHArt Conference*, ed. Tanya Szrajber, 45–62. Vol. 1. London: CHArt.

Lee, T. B. 1996. "The World Wide Web: Past, Present and Future." http://www.w3.org

Smith, A. 1996. *Software for the Self: Culture and Technology*. London: Faber.

Contributors

Jay David Bolter is the Wesley Professor of New Media in the School of Literature, Communications, and Culture of the Georgia Institute of Technology. He is the author of *Storyspace*, a program for creating hypertexts, *Turing's Man: Western Culture in the Computer Age*, and, with Richard Grusin, *Remediation*, published by the MIT Press in 1999.

Sean Cubitt is Reader in Video and Media Studies and head of Screen Studies at Liverpool John Moores University. He is author of *Timeshift: On Video Culture* (Routledge), *Videography: Video Media as Art and Culture* (Macmillan), and *Digital Aesthetics* (Sage). Chair of the Foundation for Art and Creative Technology, he has published widely on contemporary arts and media.

Jodi Dean is assistant professor of political theory at Hobart and William Smith Colleges in Geneva, N.Y. Her most recent book is *Aliens in America: Conspiracy Cultures from Outerspace to Cyberspace*. She has edited symposia on networked communications and new technologies for *Constellations* and *Signs*. Currently, she is editing a collection on Political Theory and Cultural Studies for Cornell University Press and a book on the links between conspiracy and the Internet.

Dawn Dietrich is Associate Professor of English at Western Washington University. A specialist in literature and technology, performance studies, and critical theory, she has published articles in journals such as *Word & Image: A Journal of Visual/Verbal Enquiry*; *Contemporary Literature*; *Interfaces: Image, Text, Language*; *and Arena Journal*. She is currently at work on a book about technology and postmodern performance.

Cynthia Fuchs is Associate Professor of English and Film & Media Studies at George Mason University. She is also a film and media columnist for *Philadelphia City Paper* and the on-line magazine *Pop Matters*. She is coeditor *of Between the Sheets, in the Streets: Queer, Lesbian, and Gay Documentary* (University of Minnesota Press), and is writing a book on contemporary youth and hiphop cultures.

Bruce Horner is Associate Professor of English at Drake University. He is the author of *Terms of Work for Composition: A Materialist Critique* (SUNY). He is also coeditor, with Thomas Swiss, of *Key Terms in Popular Music and Culture* (Blackwell, 1999).

Matthew G. Kirschenbaum is Assistant Professor of English at the University of Kentucky, where he teaches media studies, informatics, and contemporary literature. He divides his time between critical writing about digital culture and new media, and applied research in humanities computing.

Timothy W. Luke, Endowment Professor at Virginia Tech, teaches political science. His most recent book is *Ecocritique: Contesting the Politics of Nature, Economy, and Culture* (University of Minnesota Press, 1997).

Vincent Mosco is Professor of Communication at Carleton University in Ottawa. He is the author of four books and editor or coeditor of seven on media, communication, and new technologies. His most recent book, *The Political Economy of Communication* (Sage, 1996) draws on current work in sociology, geography, and cultural studies to rethink this approach to media studies.

Lisa Nakamura is Assistant Professor of English at Sonoma State University, where she teaches postcolonial literature and critical theory. She is coeditor of a collection entitled *Race in Cyberspace* (Routledge, 1999). She is also working on a book on Cyber-Orientalism and the Internet. Her articles on cross-racial passing and impersonation on-line have appeared in many publications.

Russell A. Potter, who teaches at Rhode Island College, is the author of *Spectacular Vernaculars: Hip-Hop and the Politics of Postmodernism* (SUNY, 1995). He is a contributor to several recent books, including *The Cambridge Companion to Rock and Pop.*

Rob Shields is editor of the journal *Space and Culture* and author of *Places on the Margin: Alternative Geographies of Modernity* (1989) and *Lefebvre: Love and Struggle—Spatial Dialectics* (1998). He is Acting Director of the Institute of Interdisciplinary Studies, and Associate Professor in Sociology and Anthropology at Carleton University, Ottawa, Canada.

John M. Sloop, Vanderbilt University, is author of *The Cultural Prison* (University of Alabama), and coeditor of two volumes, *Mapping The Beat* (Blackwell) and *Judgment Calls* (Westview Press). His work generally focuses on metacritical issues in rhetorical criticism and cultural criticism of public representations.

Thomas Swiss is Center for the Humanities Professor of English and Director of the Web-Assisted Curriculum at Drake University. He is the author of two collections of poems: *Rough Cut* (University of Illinois) and *Measure* (University of Alabama). He is the coeditor of a number of books, including *Mapping the Beat: Cultural Theory and Pop Music* (Blackwell) and *The World Wide Web and Contemporary Cultural Theory: Magic, Metaphor, and Power* (Routledge).

Joseph Tabbi is editor of a collection of essays, *Reading Matters: Narrative in the New Media Ecology* (Cornell, 1997) and author of *Postmodern Sublime: Technology and American Writing from Mailer to Cyberpunk* (Cornell, 1995). He is also editor of the *Electronic Book Review*.

Index